Analyzing Syntax and Semantics

Virginia A. Heidinger

with technical assistance from Martin R. Noretsky

Clerc Books
Gallaudet University Press
Washington, D.C.

Clerc Books
An imprint of Gallaudet University Press
Washington, DC 20002

Published 1984. Fourth printing 1996
Printed in the United States of America.

ISBN 0-913580-92-9

CONTENTS

CHAPTER 1 Nouns and Noun Phrases

Exercise 1 2
Exercise 2 4
Practice Test 6

CHAPTER 2 Verb Phrase Constituents

Exercise 3 10
Exercise 4 11
Practice Test 15

CHAPTER 3 Verbs and Verb Phrases

Exercise 5 20
Exercise 6 21
Exercise 7 23
Practice Test 26

CHAPTER 4 Sentence Patterns 1 and 2

Exercise 8 31
Exercise 9 33
Practice Test 37

CHAPTER 5 Sentence Patterns 3, 4, and 5

Exercise 10 42
Exercise 11 44
Exercise 12 46
Practice Test 50

CHAPTER 6 Language Analysis I
Exercise 56

CHAPTERS 1-6 Review Test 63

CHAPTER 7 Pronominalization

Exercise 13 71
Exercise 14 73
Exercise 15 74
Practice Test 77

CHAPTER 8 Sentence Complexities

Exercise 16 83
Exercise 17 84
Exercise 18 85
Exercise 19 86
Practice Test 88

CHAPTER 9 Verb Phrase Complexities

Exercise 20 92
Exercise 21 93
Exercise 22 94
Practice Test 97

CHAPTER 10 Question Modalities

Exercise 23 102
Exercise 24 104
Exercise 25 104
Practice Test 108

CHAPTER 11 Particle Movement and *There* Transformation

Exercise 26 113
Exercise 27 114
Practice Test 116

CHAPTER 12 The Passive Transformation

Exercise 28 119
Exercise 29 120
Practice Test 123

CHAPTER 13 Language Analysis II
Exercise 128

CHAPTERS 1-13 Review Test 141

CHAPTER 14 Coordination

Exercise 30 149
Exercise 31 153
Exercise 32 154
Practice Test 157

CHAPTER 15 Subordination

Exercise 33 165
Exercise 34 166
Exercise 35 167
Practice Test 170

CHAPTER 16 Relativization

Exercise 36 175
Exercise 37 177
Practice Test 183

CHAPTER 17 Comparatives

Exercise 38 192
Practice Test 196

CHAPTER 18 Language Analysis III
Exercise 200

CHAPTERS 1-18 Review Test 210

CHAPTER 19 Nominalization and Complementation

Exercise 39 218
Exercise 40 220
Exercise 41 223
Practice Test 228

CHAPTER 20 Complementation with Direct and Indirect Discourse

Exercise 42 238
Exercise 43 239
Practice Test 245

CHAPTER 21 Complementation with *Wh*-Cla[illegible] Factive Clauses, and Other Nominalizations

Exercise 44 251
Exercise 45 252
Practice Test 257

CHAPTER 22 Language Analysis IV
Exercise 264

CHAPTERS 1-22 Review Test 273

Analyzing Syntax and Semantics

CHAPTER 1

Nouns and Noun Phrases

Exercise 1

?1. Specify the features of the italicized nouns as + or −.

a. Many *people* were at the party. [+ human], [− singular], [+common], [+concrete]

b. The *pyramids* were beautiful at sunset. [− animate], [+ count], [+ concrete], [− singular]

c. Joan intends to study *law* at an eastern college. [− animate], [− count], [− concrete], [+ singular]

d. The *tiger* peered through the bars. [+ count], [+ animate], [+ singular], [+ concrete]

e. *Kevin* is Tom's brother. [+ human], [+ singular], [+ concrete], [− common]

2. a. List 3 genitive determiners.

my ______ your ______ his ______

b. List 3 articles.

a ______ each ______ every ______

c. List 3 ordinals.

first ______ second ______ third ______

d. List 3 cardinals.

one ______ two ______ three ______

e. List 3 prearticles.

just ______ only ______ even ______

f. List 3 demonstrative determiners.

this ______ that ______ these ______

3. Label each word as [+ def] or [− def].

a. this + ______

b. his + ______

c. an − ______

d. each + ______

e. enough − ______

f. four − ______

4. Circle the noun phrases in the following sentences.

   a. My last few payments are due soon.

   b. Several other events inspired the citizens.

   c. The factory offers only a few new jobs.

   d. One of those children is in the play.

5. Circle and name each type of determiner in the noun phrases below.

   a. the last two years — the: +def art, last: ord, two: card

   b. a few decisions — a: -def art, few: card

   c. even that movie — even: preart, that: dem

   d. all of these animals — all of: preart, these: dem

6. Write the symbols for the following terms.

   a. determiner — det

   b. noun phrase — NP

   c. feature — [ ]

   d. consists of — →

7. Write the phrase structure rules for each of the following noun phrases.

   a. both of his legs — preart + gen + N

   b. several of these books — preart + dem + N

   c. my third trophy — gen + ord + N

   d. those six apples — dem + card + N

8. Write a noun phrase for each.

   a. dem + ord + N — this first play

   b. gen + card + N — his two cousins

   c. preart + dem + ord + N — only that last suit

   d. def art + ord + N — the second waltz

   e. card + N — three mice

Exercise 2

1. Identify the following definitions.

   a. An affix that comes before the base form of a word. prefix

   b. The smallest unit of meaning in grammar. morpheme

   c. An affix that follows the base form of a word. suffix

   d. An addition to the base form of a word. affix

2. Specify the two types of regular inflections for nouns.

   plural possessive

3. Indicate if the italicized nouns are plural, possessive, or both.

   a. There are several *Sharons* in my class. plural

   b. The *rabbits'* ears were black. both

   c. *Mary's* sisters are nurses. possessive

   d. His *problems* were overwhelming. plural

   e. The *deer's* only food was provided by the rangers. possessive/both

4. Give the base word and the derivational affix(es) for each of the derived nouns.

   a. goodness good-ness

   b. dentistry dentist-ry

   c. hesitation hesitate -ion

   d. actor act-or

   e. honesty honest-y

Exercise 1: Answers

1. a. people:	[+human]	[−singular]	[+common]	[+concrete]
b. pyramids:	[−animate]	[+count]	[+concrete]	[−singular]
c. law:	[−animate]	[−count]	[−concrete]	[+singular]
d. tiger:	[+count]	[+animate]	[+singular]	[+concrete]
e. Kevin:	[+human]	[+singular]	[+concrete]	[−common]

2. a. my, your, his, her, its, our, their (any 3)
   b. a, an, the, some, any, enough, no, each, every, either, neither (any 3)
   c. first, second, third, last, next, etc. (any 3)
   d. one, two, many, few, several, etc. (any 3)
   e. just, only, even, both of, gallon of, one of, etc. (any 3)
   f. this, that, these, those (any 3)

3. a. [+def]
   b. [+def]
   c. [−def]
   d. [+def]
   e. [−def]
   f. [−def]

4. a. my last few payments
   b. several other events, the citizens
   c. the factory, only a few new jobs
   d. one of those children, the play

5. a. the: +def art, last: ord, two: card
   b. a: −def art, few: card
   c. even: preart, that: dem
   d. all of: preart, these: dem

6. a. det
   b. NP
   c. [ ]
   d. →

7. a. preart + gen + N
   b. preart + dem + N
   c. gen + ord + N
   d. dem + card + N

8. The following answers are examples. Your answers may vary.
   a. this first play
   b. his two cousins
   c. only that last suit
   d. the second waltz
   e. three mice

Exercise 2: Answers

1. a. prefix
   b. morpheme
   c. suffix
   d. affix

2. plural, possessive

3. a. plural
   b. both
   c. possessive
   d. plural
   e. both or possessive

4. a. good, -ness
   b. dentist, -ry
   c. hesitate, -ion
   d. act, -or
   e. honest, -y

CHAPTER 1

Practice Test

1. Specify the features of the italicized nouns as + or −.

   a. *Safety* is precautionary. [count], [concrete], [singular], [human]

   b. Tom goes away every *summer*. [count], [concrete], [singular], [common]

   c. *Bears* raided our campsite. [count], [animate], [concrete], [singular]

   d. The author was surrounded by autograph *seekers*. [count], [human], [concrete], [singular]

   e. *Sandy* is my niece. [count], [human], [singular], [common]

2. a. List 3 genitive determiners.

   __________ __________ __________

   b. List 3 articles.

   __________ __________ __________

   c. List 3 ordinals.

   __________ __________ __________

   d. List 3 cardinals.

   __________ __________ __________

   e. List 3 prearticles.

   __________ __________ __________

   f. List 3 demonstratives.

   __________ __________ __________

3. Identify the determiners as [+def] or [−def].

   a. our ______

   b. the ______

   c. any ______

   d. those ______

   e. six ______

   f. several ______

4. Circle the noun phrases in the following sentences.

   a. Both of his sisters live in Iowa.

   b. Six other peaches are in the pantry.

   c. Those two girls looked at several of the magazines.

   d. John gave many other reasons.

5. Identify and name each type of determiner in the noun phrases below.

   a. only the last names

   ____

   b. another final exam

   ____

   c. many of those people

   ____

   d. both of my children

   ____

6. Write the symbols for the following terms.

   a. determiner ______________

   b. noun phrase ______________

   c. feature ______________

   d. consists of ______________

7. Write the phrase structure rules for each of the following noun phrases.

   a. the last seven years ______________

   b. my other two brothers ______________

   c. one of his many friends ______________

   d. just these few sentences ______________

   e. every second Thursday ______________

8. Write a noun phrase for each.

   a. def art + ord + card + N

   ____

   b. dem + card + N

   ____

   c. gen + ord + N

   ____

   d. preart + dem + card + N

   ____

   e. dem + ord + N

   ____

9. Identify the following definitions.

   a. An affix that follows the base form of a word. ______________

   b. An addition to the base form of a word. ______________

   c. The smallest unit of meaning in grammar. ______________

   d. An affix that comes before the base form of a word. ______________

10. Specify the two types of regular inflections for nouns.

    ______________ ______________

11. Indicate if the italicized nouns are plural, possessive, or both.

    a. *Max's* pictures were outstanding. ______________

    b. The *frogs'* legs were broken. ______________

    c. My *puppies* are tiny. ______________

    d. The *sun's* rays are intense. ______________

    e. The *dolls'* coats were frayed. ______________

12. Identify the base word and derivational affix for each derived noun.

    a. inducement ______________

    b. silliness ______________

c. heraldry ______________________

d. construction ______________________

e. driver ______________________

Chapter 1 Practice Test: Answers

1.
a.	safety:	[−count]	[−concrete]	[+singular]	[−human]
b.	summer:	[+count]	[−concrete]	[+singular]	[+common]
c.	bears:	[+count]	[+animate]	[+concrete]	[−singular]
d.	seekers:	[+count]	[+human]	[+concrete]	[−singular]
e.	Sandy:	[+count]	[+human]	[+singular]	[−common]

2. a. my, your, his, her, its, our, their (any 3)
   b. a, an, the, some, any, no, each, every, either, neither (any 3)
   c. first, second, third, last, next, etc. (any 3)
   d. one, two, few, several, etc. (any 3)
   e. even, just, only, both of, etc. (any 3)
   f. this, that, these, those (any 3)

3. a. [+def]
   b. [+def]
   c. [−def]
   d. [+def]
   e. [−def]
   f. [−def]

4. a. both of his sisters, Iowa
   b. six other peaches, the pantry
   c. those two girls, several of the magazines
   d. John, many other reasons

5. a. only: preart, the: +def art, last: ordinal
   b. another: −def art, final: ordinal
   c. many of: preart, those: dem
   d. both of: preart, my: gen

6. a. Det
   b. NP
   c. [ ]
   d. →

7. Items a-d may end with +N or +pl + N.
   a. +def art + ord + card + N
   b. gen + ord + card + N
   c. preart + gen + card + N
   d. preart + dem + card + N
   e. +def art + ord + N

8. The following answers are only examples. Your answers may vary.
   a. the last two apples
   b. these four chairs
   c. his second try
   d. even those two pictures
   e. that first box

9. a. suffix
   b. affix
   c. morpheme
   d. prefix

10. plural, possessive

11. a. possessive
    b. both
    c. plural
    d. possessive
    e. both

12. a. induce, -ment
    b. silly, -ness
    c. herald, -ry
    d. construct, -ion
    e. drive, -er

CHAPTER 2

Verb Phrase Constituents

Exercise 3

1. List 3 types of adverbials.

   ______________ ______________ ______________

2. Write the appropriate question word (phrase) for each adverbial below.

   a. upstairs ______________

   b. tomorrow ______________

   c. annually ______________

   d. comfortably ______________

   e. shortly ______________

3. Circle all the one-word adverbials in the sentences below and specify the type of each.

   a. She often cried at night. ______________

   b. The child walked awkwardly into the room. ______________

   c. They frequently go there. ______________

   d. They met at the cafeteria openly. ______________

   e. They sometimes play inside. ______________

4. Write the symbols for the following terms.

   a. adverbial ______________

   b. preposition ______________

   c. prepositional phrase ______________

5. Circle the noun phrase or prepositional phrase adverbials in the sentences below and specify the type of each as time, frequency, etc.

   a. The children played beneath the small waterfall. ______________

   b. Every evening Tom walked around the lake. ______________

c. Tom should arrive in New York this weekend. place, time

d. Mary walks through the park each day. place, frequency

6. Circle the adverbials in each sentence and identify the form of each as one-word Adv, NP, or PP and specify the type of each.

a. Frank has been ill since last Thursday. PP, duration

b. She walked near the house. PP, place

c. Every Saturday my mother goes shopping. NP, frequency

d. The beggar moved aimlessly. one-word, manner

e. They left work quickly this afternoon. one-word manner / NP, time

7. State the order used by Fitzgerald for adverbials denoting time, manner, and place.

a. place

b. manner

c. time

8. Identify the base word and the derivational affixes used in deriving the following words.

a. carefully care-ful-ly

b. noiselessly noise-less-ly

c. happily happyily

d. shrewdly shrewd-ly

Exercise 4

1. Write the symbol used for adjective. adj.

2. State the test that you can use to determine if a word is an adjective.

Place word in the open slots in: The very ___ (noun) is very ___.

3. Circle the adjectives in the list below.

a. rough	c. grief	e. lawn	g. always	i. cloudy
b. often	d. purple	f. pure	h. grateful	j. bless

4. Circle the adjectives in the sentences below.

   a. Your friend seems tense.

   b. The movie was offensive.

   c. That arrogant cook prepared a tasteless meal.

   d. The brilliant student solved several difficult problems.

5. Define noun adjunct. a noun used as a noun modifier

6. Underline the prenominal modifier and identify it as an adjective (Adj) or a noun adjunct (NA).

a. pay period	NA	d. the rubber stamp	NA
b. the scarlet letter	Adj.	e. a harsh remark	Adj.
c. a coal mine	NA	f. her hair dryer	NA

7. Write the comparative and superlative suffixes for regularly inflected adjectives.

   -er   -est

8. Write the comparative and superlative form for each adjective.

	Comparative	*Superlative*
a. lovely	lovlier	lovliest
b. careless	more careless	most careless
c. hard	harder	hardest
d. calm	calmer	calmest
e. sleepy	sleepier	sleepiest

9. Indicate with R or IR if each of the adjectives is regularly inflected for the comparative and superlative or is irregularly compared.

a. good	IR	e. dizzy	R
b. safe	R	f. bountiful	IR
c. southern	IR	g. dry	R
d. handsome	IR		

10. For each of the adjectives give the base word from which it was derived and the derivational affix.

    a. imaginative ____________________

    b. cowardly ____________________

    c. genetic ____________________

    d. active ____________________

    e. hasty ____________________

Exercise 3: Answers

1. adverbials of place, adverbials of manner, adverbials of time, adverbials of frequency, adverbials of duration, adverbials of reason (any 3)

2. a. where
   b. when
   c. how often
   d. how
   e. when

3. a. often: frequency
   b. awkwardly: manner
   c. frequently: frequency, there: place
   d. openly: manner
   e. sometimes: frequency, inside: place

4. a. Adv
   b. Prep
   c. PP

5. a. beneath the small waterfall: place
   b. every evening: frequency, around the lake: place
   c. in New York: place, this weekend: time
   d. through the park: place, each day: frequency

6. a. since last Thursday: PP, duration
   b. near the house: PP, place
   c. every Saturday: NP, frequency
   d. aimlessly: one-word, manner
   e. quickly: one-word, manner, this afternoon: NP, time

7. a. place
   b. manner
   c. time

8. a. care, -ful, -ly
   b. noise, -less, -ly
   c. happy, -ly
   d. shrewd, -ly

Exercise 4: Answers

1. Adj

2. Place word in the open slots in: The very _______ (noun) is very _______.

3. a, d, f, h, i

4. a. tense
   b. offensive
   c. arrogant, tasteless
   d. brilliant, difficult

5. noun adjunct: a noun used as a noun modifier

6. a. pay: NA
   b. scarlet: Adj
   c. coal: NA
   d. rubber: NA
   e. harsh: Adj
   f. hair: NA

7. a. comparative: -er
   b. superlative: -est

8. a. lovelier, loveliest
   b. more careless, most careless
   c. harder, hardest
   d. calmer, calmest
   e. sleepier, sleepiest

9. a. IR
   b. R
   c. IR
   d. IR
   e. R
   f. IR
   g. R

10. a. imagine, -ative
    b. coward, -ly
    c. gene, -tic
    d. act, -ive
    e. haste, -y

CHAPTER 2

Practice Test

1. List 3 types of adverbials.

   ______________________ ______________________ ______________________

2. Write the appropriate question word (phrase) for each adverbial below.

   a. yesterday ______________________

   b. inside ______________________

   c. quickly ______________________

   d. daily ______________________

   e. clumsily ______________________

3. Circle all the one-word adverbials in the sentences below and specify the type of each.

   a. He clumsily tripped down the stairs. ______________________

   b. Felipa occasionally studies in the library. ______________________

   c. We speedily ran home. ______________________

   d. I will read that later. ______________________

   e. He never goes outside. ______________________

4. Write the symbols for the following terms.

   a. adverbial ______________________

   b. preposition ______________________

   c. prepositional phrase ______________________

5. Circle the noun phrase or prepositional phrase adverbials in the sentences below and specify the adverbial as denoting time, manner, etc.

   a. In the evening we talked a long time. ______________________

   b. We strolled along the river every night. ______________________

   c. After the party Tom slept like a baby. ______________________

   d. Each day she stood before the mirror. ______________________

6. Circle the adverbials in each sentence and identify the form of each as one-word, NP, or PP.

   a. The dog barked throughout the night. ______________________

   b. We walked among the bright flowers. ______________________

   c. Sandy dances gracefully. ______________________

   d. Each September the school bells ring again. ______________________

   e. He sees the accountant at home. ______________________

7. State the order used by Fitzgerald for adverbials of time, place, and duration.

   a. ______________________

   b. ______________________

   c. ______________________

8. Write the base word from which each word was derived and the affix(es) attached to the base word.

   a. faithfully ______________________

   b. speedily ______________________

   c. clumsily ______________________

   d. fearlessly ______________________

9. Write the symbol used for adjective. ______________________

10. State the test that you can use to determine if a word is an adjective.

    ____

11. Circle the adjectives in the list below.

    a. angry
    b. trash
    c. usually
    d. happiness
    e. lucky
    f. again
    g. grey
    h. hold
    i. skillful
    j. tame

12. Circle the adjectives in the sentences below.

   a. The child was careless.

   b. The young actress wore a lovely dress.

   c. That needy man asked for some money.

   d. You seem uncomfortable.

   e. Two trees stood near the decrepit house.

   f. The first speaker is a lively person.

13. Define noun adjunct.

   ____

14. Underline the prenominal modifier and identify it as an adjective (Adj) or a noun adjunct (NA).

   a. a sore arm ______________________

   b. the shoe horn ______________________

   c. the chess player ______________________

   d. a terrific joke ______________________

   e. a life raft ______________________

15. Write the comparative and superlative form for each adjective.

	Comparative	*Superlative*
a. happy	______________	______________
b. handsome	______________	______________
c. sharp	______________	______________
d. lively	______________	______________
e. good	______________	______________
f. cautious	______________	______________

16. Indicate with R or IR if each of the following has a regular or irregular comparison.

   a. far ______________________

   b. hairy ______________________

c. lovely ______________________

d. faithful ______________________

e. clean ______________________

17. For each adjective below, write the base word from which it was derived and the derivational affix applied to the base.

a. humorous ______________________

b. cheery ______________________

c. resentful ______________________

d. excitable ______________________

e. neighborly ______________________

f. repulsive ______________________

Chapter 2 Practice Test: Answers

1. adverbials of place, adverbials of manner, adverbials of time, adverbials of frequency, adverbials of duration, adverbials of reason (any 3)

2. a. when
   b. where
   c. how
   d. how often
   e. how

3. a. clumsily: manner
   b. occasionally: frequency
   c. speedily: manner, home: place
   d. later: time
   e. never: frequency, outside: place

4. a. Adv
   b. Prep
   c. PP

5. a. in the evening: time, a long time: duration
   b. along the river: place, every night: frequency
   c. after the party: time, like a baby: manner
   d. each day: frequency, before the mirror: place

6. a. throughout the night: PP
   b. among the bright flowers: PP
   c. gracefully: one-word
   d. each September: NP, again: one-word
   e. at home: PP

7. a. place
   b. duration
   c. time

8. a. faith, -ful, -ly
   b. speed, -y, -ly
   c. clumsy, -ly
   d. fear, -less, -ly

9. Adj

10. Place word in the open slots in: The very ______ (noun) is very ______.

11. a, e, g, i, j

12. a. careless
    b. young, lovely
    c. needy
    d. uncomfortable
    e. decrepit
    f. lively

13. noun adjunct: a noun used as a noun modifier

14. a. sore: Adj
    b. shoe: NA
    c. chess: NA
    d. terrific: Adj
    e. life: NA

15. a. happier, happiest
    b. more handsome, most handsome
    c. sharper, sharpest
    d. livelier, liveliest
    e. better, best
    f. more cautious, most cautious

16. a. IR
    b. R
    c. R
    d. IR
    e. R

17. a. humor, -ous
    b. cheer, -y
    c. resent, -ful
    d. excite, -able
    e. neighbor, -ly
    f. repulse, -ive

CHAPTER 3

Verbs and Verb Phrases

Exercise 5

1. List the two tenses in English.

   past ________ present ________

2. Underline the verb in each sentence and write the phrase structure rule in the blanks.

   a. Both boys write home daily. pres + write
   b. The police officer calls her parents at home. pres + call
   c. Alan caught two large bass. past + catch
   d. Kitty listed her references. past + list
   e. She raced across the field. past + race

3. Identify each form of the verb as V-Ø, V-*ing*, V-*s*, V-*en*, and/or V-*ed*.

   a. approved V-ed V-en
   b. ridden V-en
   c. passes V-S
   d. clip V-Ø
   e. splitting V-ing

4. Write the specified forms for each verb.

V-Ø	V-*ing*	V-*ed*	V-*s*	V-*en*
a. hide	hiding	hid	hides	hidden
b. gather	gathering	gathered	gathers	gathered
c. cast	casting	cast	casts	cast

5. Label each italicized verb as finite (F) or nonfinite (NF).

   a. The detectives *investigated* the murder. F
   b. Jan may *want* a drink. NF

c. The children are *making* kites. NF

d. All the kittens *ran* under the shed. F

e. The television was *damaged* on the delivery truck. NF

f. Vincent has *attended* college for a year. NF

g. Those girls often *sing* in the choir. F

6. Identify each verb as regular (R) or irregular (IR) past or present.

a. glowed R

b. fell IR

c. starts R

d. checked R

e. has IR

f. entered R

g. made IR

Exercise 6

1. Label each modal auxiliary as present or past.

a. will present

b. would past

c. can pres

d. may pres

e. might past

2. Write the verb phrase for each rule.

a. pres + may + disagree may disagree

b. past + shall + direct should direct

c. past + can + creep could creep

3. Write the rules for each VP.

a. shall call pres + shall + call

b. might harm past + harm

c. would satisfy past + will + satisfy

4. Label each of the auxiliaries below as present or past.

   a. was ___past___

   b. am ___pres___

   c. is ___pres___

   d. are ___pres___

   e. were ___past___

5. Write verb phrases for the following rules.

   a. past + be + -ing + smile ___was (were) smiling___

   b. pres + be + -ing + hop ___am (is, are) hoping___

6. Write the phrase structure rules for these specific VPs.

   a. were hopping ___past + be + -ing + hop___

   b. is using ___pres + be + -ing + use___

7. Label each of the auxiliaries below as present or past.

   a. has ___pres___

   b. had ___past___

   c. have ___pres___

8. Write the -*en* form for each verb and identify each verb as regular (R) or irregular (IR).

   a. scream ___screamed R___

   b. quit ___quit IR___

   c. throw ___thrown IR___

   d. grin ___grinned R___

9. Write the rules for the following verb phrases.

   a. has spoken ___pres + have + -en + speak___

   b. had dreamed ___past have + -en + dream___

   c. had liked ___past have + -en + like___

10. Write the verb phrase for each rule.

a. pres + have + -en + follow — have/has followed

b. past + have + -en + resist — had resisted

Exercise 7

1. Write the VPs for the following.

a. pres + may + be + -ing + slide — may be sliding

b. past + can + have + -en + know — could have known

c. past + will + have + -en + hold — would have held

2. Identify the tense of each VP as present or past and the type of auxiliary(ies) in each as *be*, modal, or *have*.

a. must be working — pres modal, be

b. has studied — pres have

c. were going — past be

d. can sing — pres modal

e. should have ended — past modal have

3. Specify the tense and aspect of each verb phrase.

	Tense	*Aspect*
a. is chattering	present	progressive
b. had been following	past	perfect progressive
c. are leaving	present	prog
d. has flown	present	perf.
e. were concealing	past	progressive

4. Specify the inflectional affix of each verb as the past, progressive, or the third singular morpheme.

a. transposes — Third singular

b. converging — prog

c. melted — past

d. grinned — past

e. singing — prog

Exercise 5: Answers

1. present, past

2. a. write: pres + write
   b. calls: pres + call
   c. caught: past + catch
   d. listed: past + list
   e. raced: past + race

3. a. V-ed and V-en
   b. V-en
   c. V-s
   d. V-Ø
   e. V-ing

4. a. hiding, hid, hides, hidden
   b. gathering, gathered, gathers, gathered
   c. casting, cast, casts, cast

5. a. F
   b. NF
   c. NF
   d. F
   e. NF
   f. NF
   g. F

6. a. R, past
   b. IR, past
   c. R, present
   d. R, past
   e. IR, present
   f. R, past
   g. IR, past

Exercise 6: Answers

1. a. present
   b. past
   c. present
   d. present
   e. past

2. a. may disagree
   b. should direct
   c. could creep

3. a. pres + shall + call
   b. past + may + harm
   c. past + will + satisfy

4. a. past
   b. present
   c. present
   d. present
   e. past

5. a. was (were) smiling
   b. am (is, are) hopping

6. a. past + be + -ing + hop
   b. pres + be + -ing + use

7. a. present
   b. past
   c. present

8. a. screamed, R
   b. quit, IR
   c. thrown, IR
   d. grinned, R

9. a. pres + have + -en + speak
   b. past + have + -en + dream
   c. past + have + -en + like

10. a. have/has followed
    b. had resisted

Exercise 7: Answers

1. a. may be sliding
   b. could have known
   c. would have held

2. a. pres, modal, *be*
   b. pres, *have*
   c. past, *be*
   d. pres, modal
   e. past, modal, *have*

3. a. present, progressive
   b. past, perfect progressive
   c. present, progressive
   d. present, perfect
   e. past, progressive

4. a. third singular
   b. progressive
   c. past
   d. past
   e. progressive

CHAPTER 3

Practice Test

1. List the two tenses in English. ____________ ____________

2. Underline the verb in each sentence and write the phrase structure rule in the blank.

   a. Paul combed his hair. ____________

   b. My aunt drove the old car. ____________

   c. The seals eat fish in the morning. ____________

   d. That child plays every afternoon. ____________

   e. She hopped over the straight lines. ____________

3. Identify each form of the verb as V-Ø, V-*ing*, V-*s*, V-*en*, and/or V-*ed*.

   a. smelled ____________

   b. won ____________

   c. answers ____________

   d. leaping ____________

   e. take ____________

4. Write the specified forms for each verb.

V-Ø	V-*ing*	V-*ed*	V-*s*	V-*en*
a. sweep	____________	____________	____________	____________
b. doubt	____________	____________	____________	____________
c. bite	____________	____________	____________	____________

5. Label each italicized verb as finite or nonfinite.

   a. Jorge has *worked* for three deans. ____________

   b. The journalist *wrote* a story about pollution. ____________

   c. I am *talking* on the telephone. ____________

d. Saccharin may *cause* cancer. ____________________

e. Eddie *rides* his bike to work. ____________________

6. Identify each verb as regular (R) or irregular (IR).

a. watch ________ d. fix ________ g. understand ________

b. display ________ e. do ________ h. buy ________

c. meet ________ f. turn ________

7. Label each modal auxiliary as present or past.

a. will ________ d. might ________

b. must ________ e. can ________

c. shall ________

8. Write the verb phrase for each rule.

a. pres + may + teach ____________________

b. past + will + draw ____________________

c. past + can + swim ____________________

9. Write the phrase structure rules for each VP.

a. might improve ____________________

b. can conduct ____________________

c. would send ____________________

10. Label each of the auxiliaries below as present or past.

a. was ________ d. are ________

b. am ________ e. were ________

c. is ________

11. Write verb phrases for the following rules.

a. past + be + -ing + display ____________________

b. pres + be + -ing + stop ____________________

12. Write the phrase structure rules for these specific VPs.

    a. was leaving ______________________________

    b. am dreaming ______________________________

13. Label each of the auxiliaries below as present or past.

    a. have ______________

    b. had ______________

    c. has ______________

14. Write the *-en* form for each verb and identify each as regular (R) or irregular (IR).

    a. forget ______________

    b. choose ______________

    c. talk ______________

    d. figure ______________

15. Write the rules for the following phrases.

    a. had taught ______________________________

    b. has watched ______________________________

    c. have blown ______________________________

16. Write the verb phrase for each rule.

    a. past + have + -en + report ______________________________

    b. pres + have + -en + lease (they) ______________________________

17. Specify the tense and aspect of each verb phrase.

	Tense	*Aspect*
a. are expecting	______________	______________
b. have been swimming	______________	______________
c. had believed	______________	______________
d. am hesitating	______________	______________
e. were swearing	______________	______________

18. In the following verb phrases identify the tense as present (pres) or past, and state the type(s) of auxiliary in each as *be*, modal, or *have*.

    a. should have written ______________________

    b. am drinking ______________________

    c. will leave ______________________

    d. had arrived ______________________

    e. may be studying ______________________

19. Write the VPs for the following.

    a. past + will + be + -ing + make ______________________

    b. pres + may + have + -en + write ______________________

    c. past + can + have + -en + speak ______________________

20. Specify the inflectional affix of each verb as the past, progressive, or third singular.

    a. pushing ______________________

    b. loved ______________________

    c. conspires ______________________

    d. lifted ______________________

    e. loses ______________________

Chapter 3 Practice Test: Answers

1. present, past

2. a. combed: past + comb
   b. drove: past + drive
   c. eat: pres + eat
   d. plays: pres + play
   e. hopped: past + hop

3. a. V-ed and V-en
   b. V-ed and V-en
   c. V-s
   d. V-ing
   e. V-Ø

4. a. sweeping, swept, sweeps, swept
   b. doubting, doubted, doubts, doubted
   c. biting, bit, bites, bitten

5. a. nonfinite
   b. finite
   c. nonfinite
   d. nonfinite
   e. finite

6. a. R
   b. R
   c. IR
   d. R
   e. IR
   f. R
   g. IR
   h. IR

7. a. present
   b. present
   c. present
   d. past
   e. present

8. a. may teach
   b. would draw
   c. could swim

9. a. past + may + improve
   b. pres + can + conduct
   c. past + will + send

10. a. past
    b. present
    c. present
    d. present
    e. past

11. a. was (were) displaying
    b. am (is, are) stopping

12. a. past + be + -ing + leave
    b. pres + be + -ing + dream

13. a. present
    b. past
    c. present

14. a. forgotten: IR
    b. chosen: IR
    c. talked: R
    d. figured: R

15. a. past + have + -en + teach
    b. pres + have + -en + watch
    c. pres + have + -en + blow

16. a. had reported
    b. have leased

17. a. present, progressive
    b. present, perfect progressive
    c. past, perfect
    d. present, progressive
    e. past, progressive

18. a. past, modal, *have*
    b. pres, *be*
    c. pres, modal
    d. past, *have*
    e. pres, modal, *be*

19. a. would be making
    b. may have written
    c. could have spoken

20. a. progressive
    b. past
    c. third singular
    d. past
    e. third singular

CHAPTER 4
Sentence Patterns 1 and 2

Exercise 8

1. State the meaning of an arrow in a formula. ______________________________

2. Write two formulas for a sentence. ______________________________

____

3. Write the formula for Pattern 1 sentences. ______________________________

4. State the meaning of the parentheses around the final constituent in the formula. ______________

____

5. Use slash bars to divide each sentence into its constituents and label each constituent.

   a. The police have been searching all day.

   b. The ghost vanished in the darkness.

   c. The Maine sank in 1898.

   d. A lot of crabgrass grows in their yard.

   e. That singer entertains in Las Vegas.

   f. Several of the ambassadors will meet tomorrow.

6. Use slash bars to divide each sentence into its constituents and label each constituent.

   a. We sat down in the cafeteria.

   b. The noise kept up throughout the night.

   c. That dog rolls over on command.

   d. Marsha passed out at the doctor's office.

   e. The students caught on quickly.

   f. My aunt dropped in after the show.

7. Identify the semantic relationships of the underlined nouns and verbs and adverbials.

   a. The baby crawled under the bed.

   ______ ______ ______

   b. The ice melted slowly.

   ______ ______ ______

   c. The engine stalled.

   ______ ______

   d. Jim learns slowly.

   ______ ______ ______

   e. The rabbits hopped through the garden.

   ______ ______ ______

   f. Tanya daydreams in school.

   ______ ______ ______

   g. That boy studied all night.

   ______ ______ ______

   h. The car is deteriorating.

   ______ ______

   i. Dad laughed about the situation.

   ______ ______ ______

   j. This baby can hear.

   ______ ______

   k. The dog rolled over.

   ______ ______

   l. The girls remained in the gym for an hour.

   ______ ______ ______ ______

Exercise 9

1. Write the formula for a Pattern 2 sentence. ____________________

2. Use slashes to divide each sentence into its constituents and label the constituents as NP^1, NP^2, (Adv).

   a. The mechanic fixed the car.

   b. That elephant ate the peanuts from my hand.

   c. Aunt Betty praised the children's efforts yesterday.

   d. The officials will hang the murderer at noon.

   e. The children feared the dark.

3. State the term used for NP^2 in traditional grammar. ____________________

4. Specify the feature(s) that nouns must have to be used as indirect objects.

   ____

5. List two prepositions that introduce phrases containing indirect objects.

   ____________________ ____________________

6. Underline and identify the NPs in the sentence that are subjects (S), direct objects (DO), or indirect objects (IO).

   a. Barry tossed the ball to his friend.

   b. Jill cleaned up the house for her mother.

   c. That police officer handed a ticket to my father.

   d. The lecturer showed a foreign film to the group.

   e. Uncle Bill bought skates for the children.

   f. Ed baked a cake for the party.

   g. Charlene received an award for bravery.

7. Analyze the pattern of each sentence by marking off and labeling the constituents as NP^1, V, V_i, NP^2, Adv.

   a. The president fired his advisor yesterday.

   b. Joe fell on the playground at recess.

   c. That jockey has ridden in many races.

d. The scientists proved the equation easily.

e. The girls are joining a club this fall.

8. Mark off and label the constituents in the following VPs.

a. point out your mistakes

b. stand near the bed

c. put off the party

d. taxi onto the runway

e. take over the government

f. rise above the clouds

g. hang up your pants

h. run down the hall

9. Identify the semantic relationships in each of the following Pattern 2 sentences.

a. Helen gave the flowers to her mother.

b. The baby saw the cat.

c. Mother played canasta last night.

d. John grew a beard this semester.

e. Mr. Marker designed the house.

f. Kirsten wants a corsage for Sunday.

g. Susie pulled the cat's tail.

_______________ _______________ _______________

_______________ _______________ _______________

h. The rock shattered their windshield.

_______________ _______________ _______________

_______________ _______________ _______________

i. Jim's band plays jazz.

_______________ _______________ _______________

_______________ _______________ _______________

j. Frank pushed Al off the porch.

_______________ _______________ _______________ _______________

k. Insects have antennae.

_______________ _______________ _______________

Exercise 8: Answers

1. An → means may be written as or consists of.

2. a. S → NP + VP
   b. S → Subject + Predicate

3. NP + V_i + (Adv)

4. that sentence constituent is optional in the pattern

5. a. NP V_i Adv
   The police / have been searching / all day.
   b. NP V_i Adv
   The ghost / vanished / in the darkness.
   c. NP V_i Adv
   The Maine / sank / in 1898.
   d. NP V_i Adv
   A lot of crabgrass / grows / in their yard.
   e. NP V_i Adv
   That singer / entertains / at Las Vegas.
   f. NP V_i Adv
   Several of the ambassadors / will meet / tomorrow.

6. a. NP V_i Adv
   We / sat down / in the cafeteria.
   b. NP V_i Adv
   The noise / kept up / throughout the night.
   c. NP V_i Adv
   That dog / rolls over / on command.
   d. NP V_i Adv
   Marsha / passed out / at the doctor's office.
   e. NP V_i Adv
   The students / caught on / quickly.
   f. NP V_i Adv
   My aunt / dropped in / after the show.

7. a. Mover—action—location
   b. Patient—process—manner
   c. Patient—process
   d. Experiencer—process—manner
   e. Mover—action—location
   f. Experiencer—process—location
   g. Experiencer—process—duration
   h. Patient—process
   i. Mover—action—reason
   j. Experiencer—process
   k. Mover—action
   l. Entity—stative—location—duration

Exercise 9: Answers

1. $NP^1 + V + NP^2 + (Adv)$

NP^1 V NP^2
2. a. The mechanic / fixed / the car.
NP^1 V NP^2 Adv
b. That elephant / ate / the peanuts / from my hand.
NP^1 V NP^2 Adv
c. Aunt Betty / praised / the children's efforts / yesterday.
NP^1 V NP^2 Adv
d. The officials / will hang / the murderer / at noon.
NP^1 V NP^2
e. The children / feared / the dark.

3. Direct object

4. [+human] or [+animate]

5. to, for

6. a. Barry: S, the ball: DO, his friend: IO
b. Jill: S, the house: DO
c. That police officer: S, a ticket: DO, my father: IO
d. The lecturer: S, a foreign film: DO, the group: IO
e. Uncle Bill: S, skates: DO, the children: IO
f. Ed: S, a cake: DO
g. Charlene: S, an award: DO

NP^1 V NP^2 Adv
7. a. The president / fired / his advisor / yesterday.
NP V_i Adv Adv
b. Joe / fell / on the playground / at recess.
NP V_i Adv
c. That jockey / has ridden / in many races.
NP^1 V NP^2 Adv
d. The scientists / proved / the equation / easily.
NP^1 V NP^2 Adv
e. The girls / are joining / a club / this fall.

V NP^2
8. a. point out / your mistakes
V_i Adv
b. stand / near the bed
V NP^2
c. put off / the party
V_i Adv
d. taxi / onto the runway
V NP^2
e. take over / the government
V_i Adv
f. rise / above the clouds
V NP^2
g. hang up / your pants
V_i Adv
h. run / down the hall

9. a. Agent—action—patient—beneficiary (Helen gave the flower to mother), Possessor—process—patient (Helen has a mother)
b. Experiencer—process—complement
c. Agent—action—complement—time
d. Experiencer—process—complement—time
e. Experiencer—process—complement
f. Experiencer—process—patient—reason
g. Agent—action—patient (Susie pulled the tail), Entity—stative—part (the cat has a tail)
h. Instrument—action—patient (the rock shattered the windshield), Possessor—process—patient (they have a windshield)
i. Agent—action—complement (the band plays jazz), Possessor—process—patient (Jim has a band)
j. Agent—action—patient—location
k. Entity—stative—part

CHAPTER 4

Practice Test

1. State the meaning of the arrow in a formula.

 ____

2. Write two formulas for a sentence.

 ______________ ______________

3. Write the formula for Pattern 1 sentences.

 ____

4. State the meaning of the parentheses around the final constituent in the formula.

 ____

5. Use slash bars to divide each sentence into its constituents and label each constituent.

 a. Several of the contestants won.

 b. His family stopped at the hotel.

 c. Christopher Columbus sailed in 1492.

 d. Midge sobbed throughout the night.

 e. Mark moved to another town.

 f. The alarm has rung for several minutes.

6. Use slash bars to divide each sentence into its constituents and label each constituent.

 a. The maid cleans up at home.

 b. The convicts broke out.

 c. Stan walked out during intermission.

 d. The children lined up in the morning.

 e. She is sleeping less each night.

 f. The soil dried up.

7. Write the formula for a Pattern 2 sentence. ______________________________

8. Use slash bars to divide each sentence into its constituents and label the constituents.

   a. The students received diplomas in June.

   b. Joey found a quarter in the hall yesterday.

   c. That restaurant hired a singer.

   d. Several of the actresses told stories.

   e. My father must be cleaning the house this morning.

9. State the term used for NP^2 in traditional grammar.

   ____

10. Specify the semantic features that nouns must have to be used as indirect objects.

    ____

11. List two prepositions that introduce phrases containing indirect objects.

    __________ __________

12. Circle and identify the noun phrases in the sentences that are subjects (S), direct objects (DO), or indirect objects (IO).

    a. The office gave a retirement party for our secretary.

    b. My doctor wrote a prescription for my sister.

    c. The attorney told the bad news to his client.

    d. Dad made a birdhouse for our neighbor.

    e. Dr. Biggs played the piano for Nancy's party.

    f. That organization trains dogs for blind people.

13. Analyze the pattern of each sentence by marking off and labeling the constituents as NP^1, V, V_i, NP^2, and Adv.

    a. The politicians debated hotly throughout the evening.

    b. That store gave prizes at the grand opening.

    c. The track team will have ten meets this spring.

d. Two of the submarines are cruising in the bay now.

e. Jason spotted Marie in the crowd.

14. Mark off and label the constituents in the following VPs.

a. checked off the days

b. jump into the pool

c. creep under the table

d. rub out the ink

e. stand on the stairs

f. walked down the hill

g. tie up the package

h. stick out your tongue

15. Identify the semantic relationships in each of the following Pattern 1 and 2 sentences.

a. The runner raced along the trail.

________________ ________________ ________________

b. Sugar dissolves slowly.

________________ ________________ ________________

c. John tossed the football.

________________ ________________ ________________

d. The girls danced all evening.

________________ ________________ ________________

e. That saw won't cut paper.

________________ ________________ ________________

f. Her dog leaps through a hoop.

________________ ________________ ________________

________________ ________________ ________________

g. The winner accepted the trophy graciously.

________ ________ ________________ ________________ ________________

h. Jack admired Tracy last night.

__________ __________ __________ __________

i. The logs burned up quickly.

__________ __________ __________

j. Jean's brother studies every night.

__________ __________ __________

__________ __________ __________

k. Dad is chopping the wood with Bill's ax.

__________ __________ __________ __________

__________ __________ __________

l. Jerry makes up stories.

__________ __________ __________

m. The children are playing football.

__________ __________ __________

n. Jane broke her arm.

__________ __________ __________

__________ __________ __________

Chapter 4 Practice Test: Answers

1. → means may be written as or consists of

2. S → NP + VP   S → Subject + Predicate

3. NP + V_i + (Adv)

4. that sentence constituent is optional in the pattern

5. a. NP: Several of the contestants / V_i: won.
   b. NP: His family / V_i: stopped / Adv: at that hotel.
   c. NP: Christopher Columbus / V_i: sailed / Adv: in 1492.
   d. NP: Midge / V_i: sobbed / Adv: throughout the night.
   e. NP: Mark / V_i: moved / Adv: to another town.
   f. NP: The alarm / V_i: has rung / Adv: for several minutes.

6. a. NP: The maid / V_i: cleans up / Adv: at home.
   b. NP: The convicts / V_i: broke out.
   c. NP: Stan / V_i: walked out / Adv: during intermission.
   d. NP: The children / V_i: lined up / Adv: in the morning.
   e. NP: She / V_i: is sleeping / Adv: less / Adv: each night.
   f. NP: The soil / V_i: dried up.

7. NP^1 + V + NP^2 + (Adv)

8. a. NP^1: The students / V: received / NP^2: diplomas / Adv: in June.
   b. NP^1: Joey / V: found / NP^2: a quarter / Adv: in the hall / Adv: yesterday.
   c. NP^1: That restaurant / V: hired / NP^2: a singer.
   d. NP^1: Several of the actresses / V: told / NP^2: stories.
   e. NP^1: My father / V: must be cleaning / NP^2: the house / Adv: this morning.

9. Direct object

10. [+human], [+animate)

11. to, for

12. a. S: the office, DO: a retirement party, IO: our secretary
    b. S: my doctor, DO: a prescription, IO: my sister
    c. S: the attorney, DO: the bad news, IO: his client
    d. S: Dad, DO: a birdhouse, IO: our neighbor
    e. S: Dr. Biggs, DO: the piano
    f. S: That organization, DO: dogs

13. a. NP: The politicians / V_i: debated / Adv: hotly / Adv: throughout the evening.
    b. NP^1: That store / V: gave / NP^2: prizes / Adv: at the grand opening.
    c. NP^1: The track team / V: will have / NP^2: ten meets / Adv: this spring.
    d. NP: Two of the submarines / V_i: are cruising / Adv: in the bay / Adv: now.
    e. NP^1: Jason / V: spotted / NP^2: Marie / Adv: in the crowd.

14. a. V: checked off / NP^2: the days
    b. V_i: jump / Adv: into the pool
    c. V_i: creep / Adv: under the table
    d. V: rub out / NP^2: the ink
    e. V_i: stand / Adv: on the stairs
    f. V_i: walked / Adv: down the hill
    g. V: tie up / NP^2: the package
    h. V: stick out / NP^2: your tongue

15. a. Mover—action—location
    b. Patient—process—manner
    c. Agent—action—patient
    d. Mover—action—duration
    e. Instrument—action—patient
    f. Mover—action—location, Possessor—process—patient
    g. Beneficiary—action—patient—manner
    h. Experiencer—process—patient—time
    i. Patient—process—manner
    j. Experiencer—process—frequency, Possessor—process—patient
    k. Agent—action—patient—instrument, Possessor—process—patient
    l. Experiencer—process—complement
    m. Agent—action—complement
    n. Agent—action—patient, Entity—stative—part

CHAPTER 5

Sentence Patterns 3, 4, and 5

Exercise 10

1. Write the formula for a Pattern 3 sentence.

____

2. Identify the tense of the following verb phrases.

   a. are ____________________

   b. must be ____________________

   c. is ____________________

   d. were ____________________

   e. should have been ____________________

3. Identify the *be* verb in each sentence as finite (F) or nonfinite (NF).

   a. Dan could be tired. ____________

   b. The boys are mischievous. ____________

   c. Mother may have been ill. ____________

   d. Our collie was beautiful. ____________

4. Write verb phrases for each of the following.

   a. pres + have + -en + be ____________________

   b. past + have + -en + be ____________________

   c. past + shall + be ____________________

   d. past + modal + be ____________________

   e. pres + modal + be ____________________

5. Analyze each Pattern 3 sentence by marking off and labeling the constituents.

   a. The violin sounded melodious.

   b. The plants grew tall in the greenhouse.

c. The water is clear near Barbados.

d. The children have been eager all day.

e. Joe seemed happy in school.

6. Analyze each sentence by marking off and labeling the constituents.

a. The trees swayed during the storm.

b. A thesaurus might have been useful.

c. Elsie felt all the towels on that shelf.

d. The farmer uses his truck every day.

e. The typist felt sick this morning.

7. Identify the pattern of each sentence as 1, 2, or 3.

a. The team must remain in Baltimore all weekend. ______

b. The bread tastes stale. ______

c. The cook tasted the pudding. ______

d. The coach remained cool during the game. ______

e. The gong sounded loud. ______

f. The teller sounded an alarm. ______

8. Identify the semantic relationships in the following sentences.

a. The children became cold outdoors.

______ ______ ______ ______

b. The soup tastes salty every day.

______ ______ ______ ______

c. The baby must be tiny.

______ ______ ______

d. The cloudy sky turned pink at dusk.

______ ______ ______ ______

______ ______ ______

e. The box should be rectangular.

________________ ________________ ________________

f. That dress is expensive.

________________ ________________ ________________

g. The frame seems square.

________________ ________________ ________________

h. The answer was intelligent.

________________ ________________ ________________

i. Lian's mother looks ancient.

________________ ________________ ________________

________________ ________________ ________________

Exercise 11

1. Write the formula for a Pattern 4 sentence.

____

2. Analyze each Pattern 4 sentence by marking off and labeling the constituents.

   a. That child becomes a tyrant without sleep.

   b. The drizzle turned into a rainstorm yesterday.

   c. That butler may have been a liar.

   d. The children were being monsters this morning.

   e. William remained a newscaster.

3. Circle and identify the noun phrases that are direct objects (DO), indirect objects (IO), and predicate nominatives (PN).

   a. Another man may become president next year.

   b. Jerry made some soup for his mother.

   c. The girls had been roommates last year.

   d. That man could be a criminal.

   e. Some woman offered ice cream to the child.

f. David changed into the Incredible Hulk before their eyes.

g. Those girls appear enemies during their arguments.

4. Identify the pattern of each sentence as 1, 2, 3, or 4 and analyze each sentence and label the constituents.

a. The scarecrow scared away the blackbirds. ____________

b. The men remained friends after the fight. ____________

c. Marsha stared pensively at the painting. ____________

d. His arm bled all evening. ____________

e. The caterpillars will become butterflies soon. ____________

f. That woman may be our mayor next year. ____________

g. The child appears lazy sometimes. ____________

5. Identify the semantic relationships expressed in each sentence.

a. Michael remained a nurse for years.

____________ ____________ ____________ ____________

b. Dad became a doctor in 1950.

____________ ____________ ____________ ____________

c. Our teacher turned into an ogre.

____________ ____________ ____________

____________ ____________ ____________

d. That old man must be a bigot.

____________ ____________ ____________

____________ ____________ ____________

e. The fur coat could have been a gift.

____________ ____________ ____________

____________ ____________ ____________

f. The gift was a lunch box.

____________ ____________ ____________

____________ ____________ ____________

Exercise 12

1. Write the formula for a Pattern 5 sentence.

____

2. Analyze each Pattern 5 sentence by marking off and labeling the constituents.

   a. Six of the birds were on the pole.

   b. The secretary could be in the other office.

   c. The president will be at the meeting in an hour.

   d. Jose should have been at school today.

   e. The two pandas have been in our zoo several years.

3. Identify the pattern of each sentence as 1, 2, 3, 4, or 5 and mark off and label the constituents.

   a. Tony had been jealous during the party. ______________________

   b. The group sang songs throughout the evening. ______________________

   c. Your invention will be a help to the workers. ______________________

   d. The child seemed upset after the fire. ______________________

   e. Mother gripped the leash tightly. ______________________

   f. The professor explained his theories to the class. ______________________

   g. Colonists arrived in the 1600s. ______________________

   h. Antonia has been downstairs all morning. ______________________

4. Write the semantic relationships in these Pattern 5 sentences.

   a. This spray is for fleas.

   ____________ ____________ ____________

   b. The thief is in jail.

   ____________ ____________ ____________

   c. Paula's party should be on Saturday.

   ____________ ____________ ____________

   ____________ ____________ ____________

d. The tiny birds may be on that limb.

__________ __________ __________

__________ __________ __________

e. The scarf is for Aunt Renee.

__________ __________ __________

f. Mr. Black could be at the conference for three days.

__________ __________ __________ __________

g. That chocolate cake was for the sale.

__________ __________ __________

__________ __________ __________

h. The convention must have been in New York that year.

__________ __________ __________ __________

Exercise 10: Answers

1. NP + V_L + Adj + (Adv)

2. a. pres
   b. pres
   c. pres
   d. past
   e. past

3. a. be, NF
   b. are, F
   c. been, NF
   d. was, F

4. a. has/have been
   b. had been
   c. should be
   d. could (would, should, might) be
   e. can (will, must, may, shall) be

5. a. NP V_L Adj
   The violin / sounded / melodious.
   b. NP V_L Adj Adv
   The plants / grew / tall / in the greenhouse.
   c. NP V_L Adj Adv
   The water / is / clear / near Barbados.
   d. NP V_L Adj Adv
   The children / have been / eager / all day.
   e. NP V_L Adj Adv
   Joe / seemed / happy / in school.

6. a. NP V_i Adv
   The trees / swayed / during the storm.
   b. NP V_L Adj
   A thesaurus / might have been / useful.
   c. NP V NP2 Adv
   Elsie / felt / all the towels / on that shelf.
   d. NP1 V NP2 Adv
   The farmer / uses / his truck / every day.
   e. NP V_L Adj Adv
   The typist / felt / sick / this morning.

7. a. 1
   b. 3
   c. 2
   d. 3
   e. 3
   f. 2

8. a. Entity—stative—condition—location
   b. Entity—stative—condition—frequency
   c. Entity—stative—size
   d. Entity—stative—color—time
      (sky turn pink dusk),
      Entity—stative—condition (sky be cloudy)
   e. Entity—stative—shape
   f. Entity—stative—quality
   g. Entity—stative—shape
   h. Entity—stative—quality
   i. Entity—stative—age (Mother look ancient),
      Possessor—process—patient (Jane have mother)

Exercise 11: Answers

1. $NP^1 + V_L + NP^1 + (Adv)$

2. a. NP^1 — V_L — NP^1 — Adv
   That child / becomes / a tyrant / without sleep.
   b. NP^1 — V_L — NP^1 — Adv
   The drizzle / turned into / a rainstorm / yesterday.
   c. NP^1 — V_L — NP^1
   That butler / may have been / a liar.
   d. NP^1 — V_L — NP^1 — Adv
   The children / were being / monsters / this morning.
   e. NP^1 — V_L — NP^1
   William / remained / a newscaster.

3. a. president: PN
   b. some soup: DO, his mother: IO
   c. roommates: PN
   d. a criminal: PN
   e. ice cream: DO, the child: IO
   f. the Incredible Hulk: PN
   g. enemies: PN

4. a. NP^1 — V — NP^2
   2, The scarecrow / scared away / the blackbirds.
   b. NP^1 — V_L — NP^1 — Adv
   4, The men / remained / friends / after the fight.
   c. NP — V_i — Adv — Adv
   1, Marsha / stared / pensively / at the painting.
   d. NP — V_i — Adv
   1, His arm / bled / all evening.
   e. NP^1 — V_L — NP^1 — Adv
   4, The caterpillars / will become / butterflies / soon.
   f. NP^1 — V_L — NP^1 — Adv
   4, That woman / may be / our mayor / next year.
   g. NP — V_L — Adj — Adv
   3, The child / appears / lazy / sometimes.

5. a. Entity—stative—equivalent—duration
   b. Entity—stative—equivalent—time
   c. Entity—stative—equivalent,
      Possessor—process—patient
   d. Entity—stative—equivalent,
      Entity—stative—age
   e. Entity—stative—equivalent
      (coat be gift)
      Entity—stative—equivalent (coat be fur),
   f. Entity—stative—equivalent (gift be box)
      Entity—stative—reason (box be [for] lunch),

Exercise 12: Answers

1. NP + V_{be} + Adv + (Adv)

2.
    NP V_{be} Adv
    a. Six of the birds / were / on the pole.

    NP V_{be} Adv
    b. The secretary / could be / in the other office.

    NP V_{be} Adv Adv
    c. The president / will be / at the meeting / in an hour.

    NP V_{be} Adv Adv
    d. Jose / should have been / at school / today.

    NP V_{be} Adv Adv
    e. The two pandas / have been / in our zoo / several years.

3.
    NP V_L Adj Adv
    a. 3, Tony / had been / jealous / during the party.

    NP^1 V NP^2 Adv
    b. 2, The group / sang / songs / throughout the evening.

    NP^1 V_L NP^1 Adv
    c. 4, Your invention / will be / a help / to the workers.

    NP V_L Adj Adv
    d. 3, The child / seemed / upset / after the fire.

    NP^1 V NP^2 Adv
    e. 2, Mother / gripped / the leash / tightly.

    NP^1 V NP^2 Adv
    f. 2, The professor / explained / his theories / to the class.

    NP V_i Adv
    g. 1, Colonists / arrived / in the 1600s.

    NP V_{be} Adv Adv
    h. 5, Antonia / has been / downstairs / all morning.

4.
    a. Entity—stative—reason
    b. Entity—stative—location
    c. Entity—stative—time, Possessor—process—patient
    d. Entity—stative—location, Entity—stative—size
    e. Entity—stative—beneficiary
    f. Entity—stative—location—duration
    g. Entity—stative—reason, Entity—stative—equivalent
    h. Entity—stative—location—time

CHAPTER 5

Practice Test

1. Write the formula for a Pattern 3 sentence.

   ____

2. Identify the tense of each of the following.

   a. am ______________

   b. could be ______________

   c. may have been ______________

   d. were ______________

   e. is ______________

3. Underline the verb *be* in each sentence and identify the form of the verb as finite (F) or nonfinite (NF).

   a. Jim has been ill for weeks. ______________

   b. Those girls are attractive. ______________

   c. Tommy should be grateful. ______________

   d. That class is being good this morning. ______________

   e. The dog was ravenous. ______________

4. Write verb phrases for each of the following.

   a. pres + have + -en + be ______________

   b. past + modal + have + -en + be ______________

   c. pres + will + be ______________

   d. past + modal + be ______________

   e. pres + can + be ______________

5. Analyze the pattern of each sentence by marking off and labeling the constituents.

   a. Helen felt resentful yesterday.

b. That problem seems tricky.

c. The flowers looked lovely on the table.

d. My dinner tasted peculiar.

e. The lion was cowardly.

6. Analyze each sentence by marking off and labeling the constituents.

   a. The therapist felt weary.

   b. The chef tasted the dessert.

   c. The nurse felt his pulse.

   d. A ghost appeared at the window.

   e. Mangoes taste sweet.

   f. Mother appeared frantic this morning.

7. Write the formula for Pattern 4 sentences.

   ____

8. Analyze each sentence by marking off and labeling the constituents.

   a. Teresa was one of the winners.

   b. Dr. Miles would have been your professor.

   c. Our husbands became friends in college.

   d. Harvey remained a Democrat until 1952.

   e. Lorraine is one of the Shipley twins.

9. Circle and identify the noun phrases that are direct objects (DO), indirect objects (IO), and predicate nominatives (PN).

   a. My aunt is sending some candy to our hostess.

   b. Tom and Dick have been drinking sodas all evening.

   c. We should have put another cup of sugar in the candy.

   d. Hans has been a resident for a year now.

   e. Sue raked up all the leaves for Dad this morning.

   f. Jim and Jason have stayed friends all through college.

g. Grandma's hair turned to silver overnight.

h. The truth seems our last resort.

10. Identify the pattern of each sentence as 1, 2, 3, or 4 and mark off and label the constituents.

a. That model will become the standard this spring. ______________________

b. Mother picked up the children after school. ______________________

c. The weather remained frigid. ______________________

d. The couple ran off into the sunset. ______________________

e. The apples turned red. ______________________

f. His fever climbed steadily during the afternoon. ______________________

g. The men became friends in high school. ______________________

11. Write the formula for a Pattern 5 sentence.

____

12. Analyze the sentences by marking off and labeling the constituents.

a. A bottle of beer is in the refrigerator.

b. The students can be in class on time.

c. The children should have been at the museum by now.

d. The picnic would have been in that park.

e. Several of his opponents were in the back room.

13. Identify the pattern of each sentence as 1, 2, 3, 4, or 5 and mark off and label the constituents.

a. The stapler may be in the bottom drawer. ______________________

b. The commander gave a reprieve to the prisoners. ______________________

c. The salesman's dream ended during the recession. ______________________

d. Jean should be holding the child on her lap. ______________________

e. The waitress looks neat in her uniform. ______________________

f. The campers were hungry after the hike. ______________________

g. Our son became a missionary after the war. ______________________

h. That man is reading in the dark. ______________________

14. Write the semantic relationships in these sentences.

a. Susan remained ill all week.

__________ __________ __________ __________

b. The lamp is in the attic.

__________ __________ __________

c. Mrs. Root became a lawyer.

__________ __________ __________

d. Martha's salad looks crisp.

__________ __________ __________

__________ __________ __________

e. That suitcase is huge.

__________ __________ __________

f. Brunch will be at noon.

__________ __________ __________

g. Herman turned into a tyrant this year.

__________ __________ __________ __________

h. That case of soda is for the picnic.

__________ __________ __________

i. This gift should be for Father for Christmas.

__________ __________ __________ __________

j. Those leaves will turn orange in the fall.

__________ __________ __________ __________

k. The moon is round.

__________ __________ __________

l. The meetings are at noon every Sunday.

__________ __________ __________ __________

m. Cordelia must have remained a nurse for 25 years.

__________ __________ __________ __________

n. The old instructor was a geneticist.

__________ __________ __________

__________ __________ __________

o. The suit material must be soft.

__________ __________ __________

__________ __________ __________

p. Her brother has been sickly for months.

__________ __________ __________ __________

__________ __________ __________

q. Mimi saw a lovely party dress yesterday.

__________ __________ __________ __________

__________ __________ __________

__________ __________ __________

Chapter 5 Practice Test: Answers

1. NP + V_L + Adj + (Adv)

2. a. pres
   b. past
   c. pres
   d. past
   e. pres

3. a. been, NF
   b. are, F
   c. be, NF
   d. being, NF
   e. was, F

4. a. have/has been
   b. could (would, might, should) have been
   c. will be
   d. should (would, could, might) be
   e. can be

5. a. (NP) Helen / (V_L) felt / (Adj) resentful / (Adv) yesterday.
   b. (NP) That problem / (V_L) seems / (Adj) tricky.
   c. (NP) The flowers / (V_L) looked / (Adj) lovely / (Adv) on the table.
   d. (NP) My dinner / (V_L) tasted / (Adj) peculiar.
   e. (NP) The lion / (V_L) was / (Adj) cowardly.

NP V_L Adj
. a. The therapist / felt / weary.
NP^1 V NP^2
b. The chef / tasted / the dessert.
NP^1 V NP^2
c. The nurse / felt / his pulse.
NP V_i Adv
d. A ghost / appeared / at the window.
NP V_L Adj
e. Mangoes / taste / sweet.
NP V_L Adj Adv
f. Mother / appeared / frantic / this morning.

. $NP^1 + V_L + NP^1 + (Adv)$

NP^1 V_L NP^1
. a. Teresa / was / one of the winners.
NP^1 V_L NP^1
b. Dr. Miles / would have been / your professor.
NP^1 V_L NP^1 Adv
c. Our husbands / became / friends / in college.
NP^1 V_L NP^1 Adv
d. Harvey / remained / a Democrat / until 1952.
NP^1 V_L NP^1
e. Lorraine / is / one of the Shipley twins.

. a. some candy: DO, our hostess: IO
b. sodas: DO
c. another cup of sugar: DO
d. a resident: PN
e. all the leaves: DO
f. friends: PN
g. silver: PN
h. our last resort: PN

NP^1 V_L NP^1
. a. 4, That model / will become / the standard /
Adv
this spring.
NP^1 V NP^2 Adv
b. 2, Mother / picked up / the children / after school.
NP V_L Adj
c. 3, The weather / remained / frigid.
NP V_i Adv
d. 1, The couple / ran off / into the sunset.
NP V_L Adj
e. 3, The apples / turned / red.
NP V_i Adv
f. 1, His fever / climbed / steadily /
Adv
during the afternoon.
NP^1 V_L NP^1 Adv
g. 4, The men / became / friends / in high school.

11. $NP + V_{be} + Adv + (Adv)$

NP V_{be} Adv
12. a. A bottle of beer / is / in the refrigerator.
NP V_{be} Adv Adv
b. The students / can be / in class / on time.
NP V_{be} Adv Adv
c. The children / should have been / at the museum / by now.
NP V_{be} Adv
d. The picnic / would have been / in that park.
NP V_{be} Adv
e. Several of his opponents / were / in the back room.

NP V_{be} Adv
13. a. 5, The stapler / may be / in the bottom drawer.
NP^1 V NP^2 Adv
b. 2, The commander / gave / a reprieve / to the prisoners.
NP V_i Adv
c. 1, The salesman's dream / ended / during the recession
NP^1 V NP^2 Adv
d. 2, Jean / should be holding / the child / on her lap.
NP V_L Adj Adv
e. 3, The waitress / looks / neat / in her uniform.
NP V_L Adj Adv
f. 3, The campers / were / hungry / after the hike.
NP^1 V_L NP^1 Adv
g. 4, Our son / became / a missionary / after the war.
NP V_i Adv
h. 1, That man / is reading / in the dark.

14. a. Entity—stative—condition—duration
b. Entity—stative—location
c. Entity—stative—equivalent
d. Entity—stative—condition,
Possessor—process—patient
e. Entity—stative—size
f. Entity—stative—time
g. Entity—stative—equivalent—time
h. Entity—stative—reason
i. Entity—stative—beneficiary—reason
j. Entity—stative—color—time
k. Entity—stative—shape
l. Entity—stative—time—frequency
m. Entity—stative—equivalent—duration
n. Entity—stative—equivalent,
Entity—stative—age
o. Entity—stative—quality,
Entity—stative—reason
p. Entity—stative—condition—duration,
Possessor—process—patient
q. Experiencer—process—complement—time,
Entity—stative—quality,
Entity—stative—reason

CHAPTER 6

Language Analysis I Exercise

Complete both syntactic and semantic descriptions and summaries for the following hypothetical sample. Use the sample in chapter 6 as a guide.

Language Sample

Subject: Bob

1. The baby banged some pots on the table.
2. My mother gave a spoon to the baby.
3. The spoon was old.
4. Tweetie is a little bird.
5. Tweetie was singing songs this morning.
6. Mother cleans up Tweetie's cage.
7. Janie is studying now.
8. Janie hits boys in school.

Syntactic Description

1. The baby banged some pots on the table.

   VP modulation:

   NP modulation:

2. My mother gave a spoon to the baby.

   VP modulation:

   NP modulation:

   NP elaboration:

3. The spoon was old.

   VP modulation:

   NP modulation:

4. Tweetie is a little bird.

   VP modulation:

   NP modulation:

   NP elaboration:

5. Tweetie was singing songs this morning.

   VP modulation:

   NP modulation:

6. Mother cleans up Tweetie's cage.

   VP modulation:

   NP modulation:

   NP elaboration:

7. Janie is studying now.

   VP modulation:

   NP modulation:

8. Janie hits boys in school.

   VP modulation:

   NP modulation:

Syntactic Summary

Sentences	*Frequency of Occurrence*	*Comments*
Pattern 1	______	______
Pattern 2	______	______
Pattern 3	______	______
Pattern 4	______	______
Pattern 5	______	______
Verb Phrase Modulations		
regular past	______	______
irregular past	______	______
progressive	______	______
regular third person	______	______
be auxiliary	______	______
uncontracted copula	______	______
prepositions	______	______
particles	______	______
Noun Phrase Modulations		
regular plural	______	______
articles	______	______
demonstrative	______	______
Noun Phrase Elaborations		
possessive noun	______	______
possessive determiner	______	______

Semantic Description

1. The baby banged some pots on the table.

2. My mother gave a spoon to the baby.

3. The spoon was old.

4. Tweetie is a little bird.

5. Tweetie was singing songs this morning.

6. Mother cleans up Tweetie's cage.

7. Janie is studying now.

8. Janie hits boys in school.

Semantic Summary

Noun cases	*Frequency of Occurrence*
Mover	______________
Agent	______________
Patient	______________
Experiencer	______________
Possessor	______________
Entity	______________
Equivalent	______________
Beneficiary	______________
Complement	______________
Verb cases	
Action	______________
Process	______________
Stative	______________

	Frequency of Occurrence
Modifier cases	
Size	______________
Age	______________
Adverbial cases	
Locative	______________
Time	______________

Language Analysis I Exercise: Answers

Syntactic Description

1. The baby banged some pots on the table. — $NP^1 + V + NP^2 + Adv$
   VP modulation: regular past
   preposition (*on*)
   NP modulation: +def art (2)
   −def art (*some*)
   regular plural

2. My mother gave a spoon to the baby. — $NP^1 + V + NP^2 + Adv$
   VP modulation: irregular past
   preposition (*to*)
   NP modulation: −def art
   +def art
   NP elaboration: possessive (gen) det (*my*)

3. The spoon was old. — $NP + V_L + Adj$
   VP modulation: uncontracted copula
   NP modulation: +def art

4. Tweetie is a little bird. — $NP^1 + V_L + NP^1$
   VP modulation: uncontracted copula
   NP modulation: Ø art
   −def art
   NP elaboration: adjective modifier

5. Tweetie was singing songs this morning. — $NP^1 + V + NP^2 + Adv$
   VP modulation: *be* auxiliary
   progressive (*-ing*)
   NP modulation: dem det
   Ø art (2)
   regular plural

6. Mother cleans up Tweetie's cage. — $NP^1 + V + NP^2$
   VP modulation: regular third person
   particle
   NP modulation: Ø art (2)
   NP elaboration: possessive noun modifier

7. Janie is studying now. $NP + V_i + Adv$
   VP modulation: *be* auxiliary
   progressive
   NP modulation: Ø art

8. Janie hits boys in school. $NP^1 + V + NP^2 + Adv$
   VP modulation: regular third person
   preposition (*in*)
   NP modulation: Ø art (3)
   regular plural

Syntactic Summary

Sentences	*Frequency of Occurrence*	*Comments*
Pattern 1	1	Adverbial (1)
Pattern 2	5	Adverbials (4)
Pattern 3	1	
Pattern 4	1	
Pattern 5	0	
Verb Phrase Modulations		
regular past	1	
irregular past	1	
progressive	2	
regular third person	2	
be auxiliary	2	was, is
uncontracted copula	2	was, is
prepositions	3	in, on, to
particles	1	
Noun Phrase Modulations		
regular plural	3	
articles	16	the (4), a (2), some, Ø (9)
demonstrative	1	that
Noun Phrase Elaborations		
possessive noun	1	
possessive (gen) determiner	1	

Semantic Description

1. The baby banged some pots on the table. — Agent—action—patient—location

2. My mother gave a spoon to the baby.
   Mother gave a spoon to the baby — Agent—action—patient—beneficiary
   Bob has a mother — Possessor—process—patient

3. The spoon was old. — Entity—stative—age

4. Tweetie is a little bird.
   Tweetie is a bird — Entity—stative—equivalent
   the bird is little — Entity—stative—size

5. Tweetie was singing songs this morning.	Agent—action—complement—time
6. Mother cleans up Tweetie's cage.	
Mother cleans up a cage	Agent—action—patient
Tweetie has a cage	Possessor—process—patient
7. Janie is studying now.	Experiencer—process—time
8. Janie hits boys in school.	Agent—action—patient—location

Semantic Summary

	Frequency of Occurrence
Noun cases	
Mover	0
Agent	5
Patient	6
Experiencer	1
Possessor	2
Entity	3
Equivalent	1
Beneficiary	1
Complement	1
Verb cases	
Action	5
Process	3
Stative	3
Modifier cases	
Size	1
Age	1
Adverbial cases	
Locative	2
Time	2

CHAPTERS 1-6

Review Test

1. Specify the features of the italicized noun in each sentence.

   a. *Randy* is in trouble because of his mischief. [human], [concrete], [singular], [common]

   b. Raccoons are *mammals*. [count], [human], [concrete], [singular]

   c. That *luggage* is beautiful. [concrete], [animate], [count], [singular]

   d. That student enjoys her *meals*. [singular], [concrete], [animate], [count]

   e. A lot of *rain* is expected tonight. [singular], [concrete], [count], [common]

   f. The *waiter* dropped a pitcher. [singular], [count], [concrete], [human]

   g. The *leaves* are beginning to change color. [singular], [concrete], [animate], [count]

2. Identify and name each type of determiner in the phrases below.

   a. only three representatives

   ____

   b. neither of the questions

   ____

   c. another time

   ____

   d. their final day

   ____

   e. these first few months

   ____

3. Write the verb phrases for the following.

   a. past + can + have + -en + be + -en + interpret

   ____

b. (they) pres + be + -ing + achieve

____

c. past + shall + be + -ing + work

____

d. pres + must + have + -en + eat

____

e. (he) past + be + -ing + be + -en + marry

____

4. Circle and identify the noun phrases that are subjects (S), direct objects (DO), indirect objects (IO), and predicate nominatives (PN).

   a. President Lanson will dedicate the statue next Tuesday.

   ____

   b. The Hearing and Speech Center recently acquired three audiometers.

   ____

   c. Someone gave $20,000 to Jerry Lewis for the Muscular Dystrophy Association.

   ____

   d. All of the children became monsters about 11:00 a.m.

   ____

   e. The president sent a medal to Corporal Brown.

   ____

   f. The teachers took their students to the Air and Space Museum.

   ____

   g. My sister should have been a doctor.

   ____

5. List the seven noun, verb, and adjective regular inflections, identifying each.

   a. ______________________

   b. ______________________

c. ______________________________

d. ______________________________

e. ______________________________

f. ______________________________

g. ______________________________

6. Circle the verb in each verb phrase and identify each as intransitive (I), transitive (T), or linking (L).

a. fired into the air ______________________________

b. responded sensitively ______________________________

c. made up the beds ______________________________

d. tasted bad ______________________________

e. pulled the wagon ______________________________

f. seemed lonely ______________________________

g. became sensitive to others ______________________________

h. hit Kelley in the gym ______________________________

7. Label each word in the list below as a noun (N), adjective (Adj), adverb (Adv), or preposition (P).

a. careful ______

b. canopy ______

c. strife ______

d. aptly ______

e. astute ______

f. deftly ______

g. always ______

h. floor ______

i. ascot ______

j. with ______

k. after ______

l. free ______

m. never ______

n. wet ______

8. List the designated forms.

a. three present tense modal auxiliaries

____

b. two past tense *be* auxiliaries

____

c. a present and past tense form of *have*

____

9. Identify the pattern of each sentence as 1, 2, 3, 4, or 5 and mark off and label the constituents.

   a. My doctor felt terrible yesterday. ________________

   b. The alarm went off at three. ________________

   c. Your package should be here before Friday. ________________

   d. Most of those highrises have become condominiums in the last few years. ________________

   e. Jerry's speech was interesting. ________________

   f. The train will stay here until midnight. ________________

   g. The student blamed the teacher for his mistakes. ________________

   h. Denise should have been in class for another fifteen minutes. ________________

   i. Mother has been taking Tom's temperature every hour. ________________

   j. Judy seemed disagreeable in class last night. ________________

   k. Many people were wandering down the street after dark. ________________

   l. Andre finished off the pie in minutes. ________________

10. Specify the case relationships of the italicized words as mover, agent, patient, experiencer, beneficiary, instrument, entity, equivalent, or complement.

   a. *The woman* skated on the ice.

   ____

   b. *Jenny* carved *the turkey*.

   ________________ ________________

   c. *The girls* regretted their mistake.

   ____

   d. *Philip* should be *a doctor*.

   ________________ ________________

   e. *The children* made *valentines*.

   ________________ ________________

   f. *The bird* darted about the room.

   ____

g. *Our disposal* grinds up *bones*.

____________________ ____________________

h. *Luke* hates *Russell*.

____________________ ____________________

i. *The committee* received *a citation* for its accomplishments.

____________________ ____________________

j. *The ice* melted slowly.

____

11. Identify the verb as action, process, or stative.

a. Factory noise could *deafen* the workers. ____________________

b. Stacy *slid* on the ice. ____________________

c. Roberto *hasn't been* a pilot long. ____________________

d. The boy *dreamed* all night. ____________________

e. The dog *gnawed* the table leg. ____________________

12. Identify the adverbial cases of the italicized words.

a. The medication is *for his migraines*. ____________________

b. Jim returned *home*. ____________________

c. The party will be *at noon*. ____________________

d. The boys swam *fast*. ____________________

e. Dad stayed up *until nine*. ____________________

f. Mr. Smith comes *every week*. ____________________

13. Complete a syntactic description (including the pattern) of the following sentences:

a. Frances hit my brother.

b. Bobby ran into the neighbor's house.

c. The little girls seemed brave during the storm.

d. Jane was laughing.

e. Those girls wanted some chocolate candy.

14. Write the semantic relationships expressed in the sentences in 13.

a. ______________________________

b. ______________________________

c. ______________________________

d. ______________________________

e. ______________________________

Chapters 1-6 Review Test: Answers

1. a. Randy:	[+human]	[+concrete]	[+singular]	[−common]
b. mammals:	[+count]	[−human]	[+concrete]	[−singular]
c. luggage:	[+concrete]	[−animate]	[−count]	[+singular]
d. meals:	[−singular]	[+concrete]	[−animate]	[+count]
e. rain:	[+singular]	[+concrete]	[−count]	[+common]
f. waiter:	[+singular]	[+count]	[+concrete]	[+human]
g. leaves:	[−singular]	[+concrete]	[−animate]	[+count]

2. a. only: preart, three: card
   b. neither of: preart, the: +def art
   c. another: −def art
   d. their: gen, final: ord
   e. these: dem, first: ord, few: card

3. a. could have been interpreted
   b. are achieving
   c. should be working
   d. must have eaten
   e. was being married

4. a. President Lanson: S, the statue: DO
   b. The Hearing and Speech Center: S, three audiometers: DO
   c. Someone: S, $20,000: DO, Jerry Lewis: IO
   d. All of the children: S, monsters: PN
   e. The president: S, a medal: DO, Corporal Brown: IO
   f. The teachers: S, their students: DO
   g. My sister: S, a doctor: PN

5. Noun: plural, -s; possessive, -s
   Verb: past, -ed; progressive, -ing; 3rd singular, -s
   Adjective: comparative, -er; superlative, -est

6. a. fired: I
   b. responded: I
   c. made up: T
   d. tasted: L
   e. pulled: T
   f. seemed: L
   g. became: L
   h. hit: T

7. a. Adj
   b. N
   c. N
   d. Adv
   e. Adj
   f. Adv
   g. Adv
   h. N
   i. N
   j. P
   k. P
   l. Adj
   m. Adv
   n. Adj

8. a. can, may, will, shall, must (any three)
   b. was, were
   c. have/has, had

9.
NP V_L Adj Adv
a. 3, My doctor / felt / terrible / yesterday.

NP V_i Adv
b. 1, The alarm / went off / at three.

NP V_{be} Adv Adv
c. 5, Your package / should be / here / before Friday.

NP^1 V_L NP^1 Adv
d. 4, Most of those highrises / have become / condominiums / in the last few years.

NP V_L Adj
e. 3, Jerry's speech / was / interesting.

NP V_i Adv Adv
f. 1, The train / will stay / here / until midnight.

NP^1 V NP^2 Adv
g. 2, The student / blamed / the teacher / for his mistakes.

NP V_{be} Adv Adv
h. 5, Denise / should have been / in class / for another fifteen minutes.

NP^1 V NP^2 Adv
i. 2, Mother / has been taking / Tom's temperature / every hour.

NP V_L Adj Adv Adv
j. 3, Judy / seemed / disagreeable / in class / last night.

NP V_i Adv Adv
k. 1, Many people / were wandering / down the street / after dark.

NP^1 V NP^2 Adv
l. 2, Andre / finished off / the pie / in minutes.

10. a. the woman: mover
    b. Jenny: agent, the turkey: patient
    c. The girls: experiencer
    d. Philip: entity, a doctor: equivalent
    e. The children: agent, valentines: complement
    f. the bird: mover
    g. Our disposal: instrument, bones: patient
    h. Luke: experiencer, Russell: patient
    i. The committee: beneficiary, a citation: patient or complement
    j. the ice: patient

11. a. process
    b. action
    c. stative
    d. process
    e. action

12. a. reason
    b. location
    c. time
    d. manner
    e. duration
    f. frequency

13. a. Frances / hit / my brother. $NP^1 + V + NP^2$
    Verb phrase modulation: irregular past
    Noun phrase modulation: Ø art
    Noun phrase elaboration: possessive (gen) det
    b. Bobby / ran / into the neighbor's house. $NP + V_i + Adv$
    Verb phrase modulation: irregular past, preposition
    Noun phrase modulation: Ø art, +def art
    Noun phrase elaboration: poss noun modifier
    c. The little girls / seemed / brave / during the storm. $NP + V_L + Adj + Adv$
    Verb phrase modulation: reg past, preposition
    Noun phrase modulation: +def art (2), reg plural
    Noun phrase elaboration: adj modifier
    d. Jane / was laughing. $NP + V_i$
    Verb phrase modulation: *be* aux, progressive
    Noun phrase modulation: Ø art
    e. Those girls / wanted / some chocolate candy. $NP^1 + V + NP^2$
    Verb phrase modulation: reg past
    Noun phrase modulation: dem, −def art, reg plural
    Noun phrase elaboration: noun adjunct

14. a. Agent—action—patient, Possessor—process—patient (someone have brother)
    b. Mover—action—location, Possessor—process—patient (neighbor have home)
    c. Entity—stative—condition—duration, Entity—stative—size (girl be little)
    d. Mover—action
    e. Experiencer—process—patient, Entity—stative—equivalent (candy be chocolate)

CHAPTER 7
Pronominalization

Exercise 13

1. Circle the personal pronouns in the sentences.

   a. I obeyed their orders.

   b. We joked about him.

   c. She called us at night.

   d. He took his books.

   e. It crept under the steps.

   f. You can stay longer.

2. Identify the person and number of each pronoun as 1st, 2nd, or 3rd, singular or plural.

   a. them ________________________

   b. us ________________________

   c. it ________________________

   d. you ________________________

   e. his ________________________

3. Circle the pronouns and label the case as nominative (N), accusative (A), or dative (D) in the following sentences.

   a. The mechanic sent the bill to me.

   b. She left it on the table.

   c. They pushed him out the door.

   d. We watched them in the afternoon.

   e. She left her fortune to him.

4. Write the appropriate personal pronoun for each of the following.

   a. third person feminine accusative pronoun ____________________

   b. second person singular genitive pronoun ____________________

   c. third person singular masculine nominative pronoun ____________________

   d. first person plural nominative pronoun ____________________

   e. first person singular nominative pronoun ____________________

5. Change the italicized noun phrase to the appropriate personal pronoun.

   a. *The passengers* slept through the storm. ____________________

   b. *That statement* was very immature. ____________________

   c. The dealer handed *my aunt and me* a gift. ____________________

   d. Frank gave *his professor* some old books. ____________________

   e. Mom bought *new curtains* for our apartment. ____________________

6. Underline the pronoun and circle its referent in the sentence. Identify each sentence as having forward or backward pronominalization, or both.

   a. Whenever he gives Sue a scolding, Dad feels sorry for her.

   ____

   b. The dog was large, but it was cowardly.

   ____

   c. Because the car was wrecked, Dad decided to replace it.

   ____

   d. Although the general needed more men, the army had no more to give him.

   ____

   e. After they shoveled the snow, the children had hot cocoa.

   ____

Exercise 14

1. Circle the reflexive pronouns in the sentences.

   a. We surprised ourselves by winning.

   b. The cat cleans itself frequently.

   c. Joe himself invented that machine.

   d. Our guests made the sandwiches themselves.

   e. You should not underestimate yourself.

2. Identify the person and number of each pronoun.

   a. myself ____________________

   b. themselves ____________________

   c. herself ____________________

   d. yourself ____________________

   e. ourselves ____________________

3. Write the appropriate reflexive pronoun for each of the following.

   a. third person plural reflexive ____________________

   b. first person plural reflexive ____________________

   c. second person singular reflexive ____________________

   d. third person singular masculine reflexive ____________________

   e. second person plural reflexive ____________________

4. Identify the transformation in each sentence as reflexive pronoun, reflexive intensifier, or reflexive intensifier movement.

   a. She occasionally whistles to herself. ____________________

   b. Carol and I drove the truck ourselves. ____________________

   c. The guests helped themselves to more beer. ____________________

   d. I bought a new stereo for myself. ____________________

   e. He himself can't do the work. ____________________

Exercise 15

1. Underline the indefinite pronouns in the sentences.

   a. Everybody enjoyed herself at the party.

   b. Something goes wrong for everyone sometimes.

   c. They asked that no one be late.

   d. Nobody liked our play.

   e. He likes everything anyway.

2. Write a different indefinite pronoun in each blank.

   a. The king didn't believe __________________.

   b. The teacher gave __________________ a stern warning.

   c. We really hope that __________________ gets hurt on the playground.

   d. __________________ has stolen my favorite ring.

3. Circle the demonstrative pronouns in the following sentences.

   a. Those are the wrong colors for these rooms.

   b. Stacey planned that today.

   c. I need these now.

   d. This goes in that room.

4. Identify each demonstrative as [+near] or [−near].

   a. those ______________________________

   b. these ______________________________

   c. this ______________________________

   d. that ______________________________

5. In the blanks following the paragraph indicate the noun phrase or other referent (antecedent) of each of the lettered pronouns.

   Tom and Sue waited patiently for the plane at the airport. (a) *It* was supposed to arrive at 8:30 with their parents aboard. (b) *They* heard that the plane had been delayed. (c) *This* frightened them. They were worried about their parents, especially since they had not seen (d) *them* for a long time. Tom raced to the information desk. "Was there a crash?" "Don't be alarmed at the delay," said the attendant. (e) "*This* happens often. The plane is overhead now waiting for a free runway."

a. ______

b. ______

c. ______

d. ______

e. ______

6. Identify each pronoun as personal (P), reflexive (R), indefinite (I), or demonstrative (D), listing the features appropriate to each as to person, number, gender, and distance.

   a. they ______

   b. yourselves ______

   c. everyone ______

   d. these ______

   e. mine ______

   f. that ______

   g. she ______

   h. himself ______

Exercise 13: Answers

1. a. I
   b. we, him
   c. she, us
   d. he
   e. it
   f. you

2. a. 3rd person plural
   b. 1st person plural
   c. 3rd person singular
   d. 2nd person singular and plural
   e. 3rd person singular

3. a. me: D
   b. She: N, it: A
   c. They: N, him: A
   d. We: N, them: A
   e. She: N, him: D

4. a. her
   b. yours
   c. he
   d. we
   e. I

5. a. they
   b. it
   c. us
   d. him/her
   e. them

6. a. he — Dad, Sue — her (both)
   b. The dog — it (forward)
   c. the car — it (forward)
   d. the general — him (forward)
   e. they — the children (backward)

Exercise 14: Answers

1. a. ourselves
   b. itself
   c. himself
   d. themselves
   e. yourself

2. a. 1st person singular
   b. 3rd person plural
   c. 3rd person singular
   d. 2nd person singular
   e. 1st person plural

3. a. themselves
   b. ourselves
   c. yourself
   d. himself
   e. yourselves

4. a. reflexive pronoun
   b. reflexive intensifier movement
   c. reflexive pronoun
   d. reflexive pronoun
   e. reflexive intensifier

Exercise 15: Answers

1. a. everybody
   b. something, everyone
   c. no one
   d. nobody
   e. everything

2. a. anybody/anyone/anything/everybody/ everyone/everything
   b. somebody/someone/everybody/everyone/ no one/nobody
   c. nobody/no one
   d. somebody/someone

3. a. those
   b. that
   c. these
   d. this

4. a. [– near]
   b. [+ near]
   c. [+ near]
   d. [– near]

5. a. the plane
   b. Tom and Sue
   c. that the plane had been delayed
   d. their parents
   e. planes being delayed

6. a. 3rd person plural nominative personal
   b. 2nd person plural reflexive
   c. singular indefinite
   d. plural [+ near] demonstrative
   e. 1st person singular personal
   f. singular [– near] demonstrative
   g. 3rd person singular nominative feminine personal
   h. 3rd person singular masculine reflexive

CHAPTER 7

Practice Test

1. Circle the personal pronouns in the sentences.

   a. We used it today.

   b. That car is probably hers.

   c. She gave him a note.

   d. He slept at my house.

   e. I expect them tomorrow.

   f. You are very late.

2. Circle the personal pronoun in each sentence and identify the person, number, case, and gender (when applicable) of each.

   a. Tony met her at the dance.

   ____

   b. They are mowing the grass.

   ____

   c. Consuela sent a watch to him.

   ____

   d. You are a funny person.

   ____

3. Circle the accusative pronouns in the sentences.

   a. We saw them last night.

   b. They took it into the house.

   c. He wants me to come tonight.

   d. My friend saw her yesterday.

   e. She washed the car for her brother.

4. Write the appropriate personal pronoun for each of the following.

   a. first person singular accusative pronoun ____________

   b. second person singular nominative pronoun ____________

   c. third person singular masculine accusative pronoun ____________

   d. second person plural genitive pronoun ____________

   e. third person singular feminine genitive pronoun ____________

5. Change the italicized noun phrase to the appropriate personal pronoun.

   a. The men pushed *the car* down the road. ____________

   b. The wrestler often beat *his opponents*. ____________

   c. *My grandmother* bakes cookies for the family. ____________

   d. Jeff bought a corsage for *his girlfriend*. ____________

   e. Ellen sold *the Hines family* her car. ____________

6. Underline each pronoun and circle its referent in the sentence. Identify each sentence as having forward or backward pronominalization, or both.

   a. Although the grocer was often late with deliveries, Mother continued to buy groceries from him. ____________

   b. Before he tarred the roof, the builder got a ladder. ____________

   c. Because the rocket was off course, the scientists decided to destroy it. ____________

   d. Jill was shy, but she was nice. ____________

   e. Whenever Marie walks with him, Pierre has his arm around her. ____________

7. Circle the reflexive pronouns in the sentences.

   a. I typed the paper myself.

   b. We helped ourselves to second portions.

   c. She herself made that dress.

   d. Please finish the exercises yourselves.

   e. The children dressed themselves quickly.

8. Identify the person, number, and gender (when applicable) of each reflexive pronoun.

   a. himself ______________________

   b. yourselves ______________________

   c. ourselves ______________________

   d. itself ______________________

9. Write the appropriate reflexive pronoun for each of the following.

   a. first person singular reflexive ______________________

   b. second person plural reflexive ______________________

   c. third person singular neuter reflexive ______________________

   d. second person singular reflexive ______________________

   e. third person plural reflexive ______________________

10. Identify the transformation in each sentence as reflexive pronoun, reflexive intensifier, or reflexive intensifier movement.

    a. We found ourselves out in the cold. ______________________

    b. The children grew the vegetables themselves. ______________________

    c. I myself don't believe your story. ______________________

    d. Alice developed a new career for herself. ______________________

    e. He works by himself most of the time. ______________________

11. Underline the indefinite pronouns in the sentences.

    a. Sometimes nothing goes right all day.

    b. Everyone wants something for the new office.

    c. We didn't know anything about the crime.

    d. Somebody must have seen them today.

12. Write a different indefinite pronoun in each blank.

    a. I think ______________ is wrong here.

    b. ______________ wants to do that awful job.

c. The company gave ________________ a large raise.

d. Has ________________ seen my blue tie?

13. Circle the demonstrative pronouns in the sentences.

    a. I want that over on this wall.

    b. This is the wrong edition.

    c. Yours are those on the shelf.

    d. These go in that drawer.

14. Identify each demonstrative pronoun as [+near] or [−near].

    a. this ________________

    b. these ________________

    c. those ________________

    d. that ________________

15. In the blanks following the paragraph indicate the noun phrase that is the referent (antecedent) of each of the lettered pronouns.

    Sally suspiciously eyed the strange man. Suddenly (a) he turned and grabbed (b) her. Several young shoe salesmen and two waitresses stood nearby. Sally yelled to (c) them for help. She made quite a disturbance. (d) This alerted the salesmen who were talking to the waitresses, and they ran to help (e) her. The salesmen scared the strange man away.

    a. ________________

    b. ________________

    c. ________________

    d. ________________

    e. ________________

16. Circle the pronouns in the sentences and identify the type of each as personal, reflexive, indefinite, or demonstrative.

    a. Everyone helped herself. ________________

    b. They sent no one a card. ________________

    c. This arrived for me at noon. ________________

    d. I said nothing to anyone. ________________

17. Use the following list to identify all the noun phrase elaborations and transformations in each sentence. The number following each sentence indicates the number of complexities you should find in the sentence.

Noun phrase elaborations:
1. possessive determiner
2. possessive noun modifier
3. adjective modifier
4. noun adjunct

Transformations:
5. personal pronoun
6. reflexive pronoun
7. indefinite pronoun
8. demonstrative pronoun
9. reflexive pronoun intensifier
10. reflexive pronoun intensifier movement

a. The little girl made something for her mother. (3)

____

b. They told everyone about their problems. (3)

____

c. I left my car keys in his jacket. (4)

____

d. Mother herself blames no one for Father's accident. (3)

____

e. Our aunt knitted those herself. (3)

____

f. They left it in a shady place. (3)

____

g. Jane's friends told us everything about themselves. (4)

____

Chapter 7 Practice Test: Answers

1. a. we, it
   b. hers
   c. she, him
   d. he
   e. I, them
   f. you

2. a. her: third person singular feminine accusative
   b. they: third person plural nominative
   c. him: third person singular masculine dative
   d. you: second person singular nominative

3. a. them
   b. it
   c. me
   d. her
   e. (no accusative)

4. a. me
   b. you
   c. him
   d. yours
   e. hers

5. a. it
   b. them
   c. she
   d. her
   e. them

6. a. the grocer — him (forward)
   b. he — the builder (backward)
   c. the rocket — it (forward)
   d. Jill — she (forward)
   e. Marie — her, him — Pierre (both)

7. a. myself
   b. ourselves
   c. herself
   d. yourselves
   e. themselves

8. a. third person singular masculine
   b. second person plural
   c. first person plural
   d. third person singular neuter

9. a. myself
   b. yourselves
   c. itself
   d. yourself
   e. themselves

10. a. reflexive pronoun
    b. reflexive intensifier movement
    c. reflexive intensifier
    d. reflexive pronoun
    e. reflexive pronoun

11. a. nothing
    b. everyone, something
    c. anything
    d. somebody

12. a. something/everything/nothing
    b. nobody/no one
    c. nobody/no one/everyone/everybody/someone/somebody
    d. someone/somebody/anyone/anybody

13. a. that
    b. this
    c. those
    d. these

14. a. [+near]
    b. [+near]
    c. [−near]
    d. [−near]

15. a. the strange man
    b. Sally
    c. Several young shoe salesmen and two waitresses
    d. the disturbance made by Sally
    e. Sally

16. a. everyone: indefinite, herself: reflexive
    b. they: personal, no one: indefinite
    c. this: demonstrative, me: personal
    d. I: personal, nothing: indefinite, anyone: indefinite

17. a. 3, 7, 1
    b. 5, 7, 1
    c. 5, 1, 4, 1
    d. 9, 7, 2
    e. 1, 8, 10
    f. 5, 5, 3
    g. 2, 5, 7, 6

CHAPTER 8

Sentence Complexities

Exercise 16

1. Underline all the preposed adverbials and specify the type of adverbial for each.

   a. Last season many bears bothered the campers.

   ____

   b. Yesterday Greg found some old coins in the sand.

   ____

   c. The little girl fearfully hid the matches.

   ____

   d. Around the city of Fez we saw an old wall.

   ____

   e. At 10:00 the butler brought our tea.

   ____

   f. The students sometimes slept through class.

   ____

2. Write each sentence twice, placing the adverbial in a different preposed position in each. Use . . . for unnecessary repetition of words.

   (sometimes) a. They have enjoyed swimming there.

   ____

   ____

   (modestly) b. June showed her award.

   ____

   ____

(always) c. It is raining on Mondays.

___

___

(often) d. We have gone to baseball games.

___

___

(hopefully) e. The family approached the priest.

___

___

Exercise 17

1. Define *intensifier*.

___

2. State another term used to refer to *intensifier*. ___

3. Circle the intensifier in each sentence and indicate if the word it signals or modifies is an adjective or adverb.

   a. The child handled the pencil rather clumsily. ___

   b. The man felt quite hopeless about the job. ___

   c. The tramp wore a very comical hat. ___

   d. Extremely improbable things happen to you. ___

   e. Our secretary types extremely fast. ___

4. Identify the italicized word as an adverbial or intensifier.

   a. They were acting *rather* fearless this morning. ___

   b. Rocky was *often* training for a fight. ___

   c. We walked *unusually* far today. ___

   d. Sergeant Dean yelled *hysterically* at the troops. ___

   e. The listeners were not *a bit* upset by her sermon. ___

Exercise 18

1. Specify two restrictions governing the indirect object transformation.

____

2. Indicate if the sentence is grammatical (G) or ungrammatical (UG).

   a. We mailed him a large package. _______________

   b. Marsha showed Tom it at the party. _______________

   c. I asked some help my teacher. _______________

   d. The governor granted her a pardon yesterday. _______________

   e. We vacuumed mother the house on Saturday. _______________

3. When appropriate, rewrite the sentence using the indirect object transformation.

   a. The hotel supplies clean linen for each day.

   ____

   b. She awarded a certificate to the most skilled people.

   ____

   c. He gave a bottle of perfume to his girlfriend.

   ____

   d. Harvey brought a bouquet of flowers to his wife.

   ____

   e. Tim polished the floors for our neighbor.

   ____

   f. Dr. Mack sent the Meyers to a specialist.

   ____

Exercise 19

1. Specify the form of the verb used in imperative sentences that are positive.

   ____

2. Identify those sentences that contain imperative modality changes by writing (Imp) in the blank.

   a. Digging this escape tunnel is difficult to do. ______________

   b. "I want her fired now," the boss yelled. ______________

   c. "Don't play with the toys," the salesperson warned. ______________

   d. Open your mouth for the dentist. ______________

   e. Bet on Firebird in the first race. ______________

3. Identify the following in the sentences.

   Modality change: 1. imperative
   Transformation: 2. adverbial preposing
   3. intensifier
   4. indirect object preposing

   a. You should always work a little harder. ______________

   b. Write Grandma a letter now. ______________

   c. The girls often finish their work rather quickly. ______________

   d. Feed the peanuts to the elephants very carefully. ______________

   e. Every day that man sends his wife flowers. ______________

   f. In the morning, put out the cat. ______________

Exercise 16: Answers

1. a. last season: time
   b. yesterday: time
   c. fearfully: manner
   d. around the city of Fez: location
   e. at 10:00: time
   f. sometimes: frequency

2. a. Sometimes they have enjoyed . . .
   They sometimes have enjoyed . . .
   They have sometimes enjoyed . . . (any two)
   b. Modestly, June showed . . .
   June modestly showed . . .
   c. It always is raining . . .
   It is always raining . . .
   d. We often have gone . . .
   We have often gone . . .
   e. The family hopefully approached . . .
   Hopefully, the family approached . . .

Exercise 17: Answers

1. words that qualify or stress the meaning of adjectives or adverbs

2. qualifier

3. a. rather, adverb
   b. quite, adjective
   c. very, adjective
   d. extremely, adjective
   e. extremely, adverb

4. a. intensifier
   b. adverbial
   c. intensifier
   d. adverbial
   e. intensifier

Exercise 18: Answers

1. The direct object cannot be a personal pronoun; the meaning must imply a recipient of some object rather than the receiver of assistance.

2. a. G
   b. UG
   c. UG
   d. G
   e. UG

3. b. He awarded the most skilled people a certificate.
   c. He gave his girlfriend a bottle of perfume.
   d. Harvey brought his wife a bouquet of flowers.

Exercise 19: Answers

1. base form

2. c, d, e

3. a. 2, 3
   b. 1, 4
   c. 2, 3
   d. 1, 3
   e. 2, 4
   f. 2, 1

CHAPTER 8

Practice Test

1. Underline all the preposed adverbials and specify the type of adverbial for each.

   a. Throughout the night, the rain drenched the yard. ______________________

   b. Most of the boys never are late. ______________________

   c. Tomorrow the Johnsons will leave their dog at the pound. ______________________

   d. For several hours traffic was light. ______________________

   e. Bea innocently told her story to the detective. ______________________

   f. In the Southwest, people are suffering. ______________________

2. Write each sentence twice, placing the adverbial in a different shifted position in each. Use . . . for unnecessary repetition of words.

   (normally) a. John will return his library books on time.

   ____

   ____

   (often) b. That family needs a babysitter.

   ____

   ____

   (quickly) c. The snake darted under the rock.

   ____

   ____

   (usually) d. The children are asleep by 9:00.

   ____

   ____

(sometimes) e. We enjoy chocolate milkshakes.

____

____

3. Define *intensifier*. ____________________

4. State another term used to refer to intensifier. ____________________

5. Circle the intensifier in each sentence and identify the word it signals or modifies as an adjective (Adj) or adverb (Adv).

   a. The group was quite bored by her presentation. ____________________

   b. Mary felt extremely humble before the queen. ____________________

   c. The old man walks a bit slowly. ____________________

   d. The sales agent had a rather sly manner. ____________________

   e. Her dog very savagely attacked the child. ____________________

6. Identify the italicized word as an adverbial or intensifier.

   a. The cheese looked *very* discolored. ____________________

   b. We were *usually* alarmed at his behavior. ____________________

   c. The driver was *quite* familiar with the area. ____________________

   d. The woman *angrily* slapped her husband. ____________________

   e. Jill has been *rather* obnoxious lately. ____________________

7. Specify two restrictions governing the indirect object transformation.

____

8. Indicate if the sentence is grammatical (G) or ungrammatical (UG).

   a. The carpenter made us a birdhouse. ____________________

   b. I caught my uncle the fish yesterday. ____________________

   c. We sold the girls it at the house. ____________________

   d. She gave the children their new drum. ____________________

   e. The company sent them a free sample last week. ____________________

9. When appropriate, rewrite the sentences using the indirect object transformation.

   a. Sheila sent the gifts to her father.

   ____

   b. The man drove a truck for the city.

   ____

   c. The coach sent the players to the showers.

   ____

   d. The professor donated her time for some reason.

   ____

   e. We found a new car for Tom.

   ____

10. Specify the form of the verb used in imperative sentences.

    ____

11. Identify those sentences that contain an imperative modality change by writing (Imp) in the blank.

    a. Putting those chairs in the attic was hard. ______________

    b. Jim yelled, "Don't walk under that ladder." ______________

    c. Always obey speed signs on the highway. ______________

    d. Shut off the engine before it blows up. ______________

    e. You must be out in a moment. ______________

12. Identify from the listed complexities those in each sentence. The number following each sentence indicates the number of complexities you should find in the sentence.

Modality change:	1. imperative	
Noun phrase elaborations:	2. poss determiner	
	3. poss noun	
	4. adj modifier	
	5. noun adjunct	
Transformations:	6. pers pro	11. reflex pro intens movt
	7. reflex pro	12. adverbial preposing
	8. indef pro	13. intensifier
	9. dem pro	14. indirect object preposing
	10. reflex pro intens	

a. In three days you should find out something. (3) ______

b. That shy child hides herself behind her mother's skirt. (4) ______

c. Always put everything in glass containers. (4) ______

d. She walks the dog herself very frequently. (3) ______

e. The Smiths themselves took care of their vegetable garden. (3) ______

f. Hold that somewhat loosely. (3) ______

g. Lend Larry your leather jacket. (4) ______

h. At 8:00 the yard will be dark enough for his torches. (3) ______

i. We usually buy ourselves a small gift. (5) ______

Chapter 8 Practice Test: Answers

1. a. throughout the night: duration
   b. never: frequency
   c. tomorrow: time
   d. for several hours: duration
   e. innocently: manner
   f. in the Southwest: location

2. a. Normally, John will. . .
   John will normally. . .
   John normally will. . . (any two)
   b. That family often needs. . .
   Often that family needs. . .
   c. Quickly the snake darted. . .
   The snake quickly darted. . .
   d. Usually the children are. . .
   The children are usually. . .
   The children usually are. . . (any two)
   e. Sometimes we enjoy. . .
   We sometimes enjoy. . .

3. words which qualify or limit the meaning of an adjective or adverb

4. qualifier

5. a. quite, Adj
   b. extremely, Adj
   c. a bit, Adv
   d. rather, Adj
   e. very, Adv

6. a. intensifier
   b. adverbial
   c. intensifier
   d. adverbial
   e. intensifier

7. The direct object cannot be a personal pronoun; the meaning must imply a recipient of some object rather than the receiver of assistance.

8. a. G
   b. UG
   c. UG
   d. G
   e. G

9. a. Sheila sent her father the gifts.
   e. We found Tom a new car.

10. base form

11. b, c, d

12. a. 12, 6, 8
    b. 4, 7, 2, 3
    c. 12, 1, 8, 5
    d. 6, 11, 13
    e. 10, 2, 5
    f. 1, 9, 13
    g. 1, 14, 2, 5
    h. 12, 13, 2
    i. 6, 12, 7, 14, 4

CHAPTER 9
Verb Phrase Complexities

Exercise 20

1. Identify the forms of the *do* auxiliary, identifying each as present or past.

   present: ______________________________

   past: ______________________________

2. Specify the form of the verb used with the *do* auxiliary.

   ____

3. Write the sentences using the appropriate *do* auxiliary to express emphasis or contradiction. (Do not use contractions.)

   a. Eleanor hit the robber at the bank.

   ____

   b. He stays overtime some days.

   ____

   c. Our uncle flies a small plane.

   ____

   d. They dance very gracefully.

   ____

   e. Two boys from our town won the prize.

   ____

4. List two kinds of sentences other than positive declaratives that require the *do*-support to mark the present or past tense.

   ______________________ ______________________

5. Write the following sentences as negative or as questions using *do*-support without contractions.

   a. Alice grew weary of his talk. (Negative)

   ____

b. Those women work in that factory. (Negative)

____

c. Al writes for the newspaper. (Question)

____

d. The pilot flew to California. (Question)

____

Exercise 21

1. Specify the position which *not* occupies

   a. when the verb is *be*.

   ____

   b. when there are one or more auxiliaries in the verb phrase.

   ____

2. Identify with an X the sentences for which the *do*-support would be used in changing them to the negative form.

   a. He's departing from the bus station. ______

   b. Those cats make noise all night. ______

   c. You'll drive my car today. ______

   d. They leave today for Africa. ______

   e. The rain fell heavily last night. ______

3. Change the following sentences to the negative without using contractions. Use the symbol . . . for words after the verb.

   a. This dog has been barking very loudly.

   ____

   b. We must have been talking quietly.

   ____

   c. Bill laughs at Gwen's jokes.

   ____

d. Sandy drove her car carefully.

____

e. Antiques make good conversation pieces.

____

Exercise 22

1. Write the contraction for the italicized words in each sentence.

   a. *I have* written a good story. ______________

   b. *She has* been here before. ______________

   c. *John is* next in line. ______________

   d. *They will* go to the late show. ______________

   e. *We are* having a lousy week. ______________

   f. *He had* left for New York. ______________

2. Specify the contraction in each sentence as a *have*, *be*, or modal contraction.

   a. They'd often been wrong. ______________

   b. I'll be moving along. ______________

   c. It's been a hot day. ______________

   d. She's coming home tonight. ______________

   e. We're nuns from the convent. ______________

3. Identify the contraction in each sentence as a contracted *be* verb or *be* auxiliary.

   a. Jim's a good dancer. ______________

   b. Mary's going to the party. ______________

   c. They're raising chickens this year. ______________

   d. She's not in school today. ______________

   e. They're rather fast drivers. ______________

4. Write the appropriate contraction for the italicized words in each sentence.

   a. Tessa *will not* eat her dinner. ______________________

   b. Those boys *cannot* swim. ______________________

   c. *I am* not going. ______________________

   d. The girls *are not* coming. ______________________

   e. Rosa *had not* made the beds. ______________________

   f. That boy *was not* shy. ______________________

5. Change the sentences to the negative form using contractions whenever possible. Use the symbol . . . for words after the verb or negative.

   a. I am anxious about the operation.

   ____

   b. The team will be flying to Chicago tonight.

   ____

   c. He danced very well.

   ____

   d. The bats hide in the cave.

   ____

   e. Her gas tank was leaking yesterday.

   ____

6. Identify the listed complexities in each sentence.

   Modality change: 1. negation
   Transformations: 2. *do*-support
   3. contraction

   a. Diane did not do her homework. ______________________

   b. They'll never have any money. ______________________

   c. She's had no money for food for a week. ______________________

   d. Fritz didn't go to the party. ______________________

   e. Erwin wouldn't do the dishes. ______________________

   f. I'll buy nothing in that store. ______________________

Exercise 20: Answers

1. present: do, does
   past: did

2. the base form

3. a. Eleanor did hit the robber at the bank.
   b. He does stay overtime some days.
   c. Our uncle does fly a small plane.
   d. They do dance very gracefully.
   e. Two boys from our town did win the prize.

4. negative declarative, interrogative, negative interrogative (any two)

5. a. Alice did not grow weary of his talk.
   b. Those women do not work in that factory.
   c. Does Al write for the newspaper?
   d. Did the pilot fly to California?

Exercise 21: Answers

1. a. after the verb *be*
   b. after the auxiliary carrying the tense of the VP

2. b, d, e

3. a. This dog has not been barking. . .
   b. We must not have been talking. . .
   c. Bill does not laugh. . .
   d. Sandy did not drive. . .
   e. Antiques do not make. . .

Exercise 22: Answers

1. a. I've
   b. She's
   c. John's
   d. They'll
   e. We're
   f. He'd

2. a. *have*
   b. modal
   c. *have*
   d. *be*
   e. *be*

3. a. verb
   b. auxiliary
   c. auxiliary
   d. verb
   e. verb

4. a. won't
   b. can't
   c. I'm
   d. aren't
   e. hadn't
   f. wasn't

5. a. I'm not. . .
   b. The team won't be flying. . .
   c. He didn't dance. . .
   d. The bats don't hide. . .
   e. Her gas tank wasn't leaking. . .

6. a. 2, 1
   b. 3, 1
   c. 3, 1
   d. 2, 1, 3
   e. 1, 3
   f. 3, 1

CHAPTER 9
Practice Test

1. Identify the forms of the *do* auxiliary, identifying each as present or past.

 ____

 ____

2. Specify the form of the verb used with the *do* auxiliary.

 ____

3. Write the sentences using the appropriate *do* auxiliary to express emphasis or contradiction. (Do not use contractions.)

 a. We really enjoy playing ping pong.

 ____

 b. Matt left on time.

 ____

 c. My uncle races roadsters sometimes.

 ____

 d. Some students got straight As.

 ____

 e. Everyone ignored the stop sign.

 ____

4. List two kinds of sentences other than positive declaratives that require the *do*-support to mark the present or past tense.

 ____

5. Write the following sentences as negatives or as questions using the *do*-support without contractions.

 a. Joan appeared very happy. (Negative)

 ____

b. Nate put the racket in the closet. (Question)

____

c. We like spinach salad. (Negative)

____

d. These children walk to school. (Question)

____

6. Specify the position that *not* occupies

   a. when the verb is *be*

   ____

   b. when there are one or more auxiliaries in the verb phrase

   ____

7. Put an X after those sentences for which the *do*-support would be used in changing to the negative form.

   a. We'll talk about that later. ______

   b. The man tripped on the cord. ______

   c. Those pens rolled off the desk. ______

   d. He ignores warnings. ______

8. Change the following sentences to the negative without using contractions. Use the symbol . . . for words after the verb.

   a. Frank mailed the large package.

   ____

   b. The cat has been jumping out the window.

   ____

   c. Jill enjoys baking very much.

   ____

   d. Some dogs need a lot of room to play in.

   ____

   e. She must have been eating elsewhere.

   ____

9. Write the contraction for the italicized words in each sentence.

   a. *Dad is* outside in the garage. ______________________

   b. *They are* watching a movie. ______________________

   c. *She will* swim in the next meet. ______________________

   d. *They have* finished their papers. ______________________

   e. *I am* babysitting tonight. ______________________

   f. *We are* returning. ______________________

10. Specify the contraction in each sentence as a *have*, *be*, or modal contraction.

   a. We'll arrive around 7:00. ______________________

   b. It's pouring outside. ______________________

   c. They'd captured the criminal. ______________________

   d. They're artists in New York. ______________________

   e. He's been cranky all day. ______________________

11. Identify the contraction in each sentence as a *be* verb or *be* auxiliary contraction.

   a. We're in the gym now. ______________________

   b. You're spinning your wheels. ______________________

   c. It's raining in Alexandria now. ______________________

   d. She's not upset about her grades. ______________________

   e. They're not behind in their work. ______________________

12. Write the contraction for the italicized words in each sentence.

   a. The box *is not* on that shelf. ______________________

   b. She *had not* put the car away. ______________________

   c. Sam *will not* eat potatoes. ______________________

   d. He *should not* be the president. ______________________

   e. The plants *do not* bloom in the shade. ______________________

   f. My dog *cannot* roll over. ______________________

13. Identify all the modality changes, noun phrase elaborations, and transformations in each sentence by using the numbered list. The number following each sentence indicates the number of complexities in the sentence.

Modality changes:	1. imperative
	2. negation
NP elaborations:	3. poss determiner
	4. poss noun
	5. adj modifier
	6. noun adjunct
Transformations:	7. pers pro
	8. reflex pro
	9. indef pro
	10. dem pro
	11. reflex pro intens
	12. reflex pro intens movt
	13. adv preposing
	14. intensifier
	15. indirect obj preposing
	16. *do*-support
	17. contraction

a. Don't count on him for anything. (6) ____________________

b. Those young children often bring their teacher some flowers. (4) ____________________

c. Nancy couldn't have done that herself. (4) ____________________

d. That paper crown won't mess up Mary's hair. (4) ____________________

e. You didn't hurt yourself too badly. (6) ____________________

f. Dad himself has no new clothes. (3) ____________________

g. Now put these under his bed. (4) ____________________

h. They've never sent the children their gifts. (6) ____________________

i. Ralph doesn't clean windows for anyone. (4) ____________________

Chapter 9 Practice Test: Answers

1. present: do, does
   past: did

2. the base form

3. a. We really do enjoy playing ping pong.
   b. Matt did leave on time.
   c. My uncle does race roadsters sometimes.
   d. Some students did get straight As.
   e. Everyone did ignore the stop sign.

4. negative declarative, interrogative, negative interrogative (any two)

5. a. Joan did not appear very happy.
   b. Did Nate put the racket in the closet?
   c. We do not like spinach salad.
   d. Do these children walk to school?

6. a. after the verb *be*
   b. after the auxiliary carrying the tense

7. b, c, d

8. a. Frank did not mail. . .
   b. The cat has not been jumping. . .
   c. Jill does not enjoy. . .
   d. Some dogs do not need. . .
   e. She must not have been eating. . .

9. a. Dad's
   b. They're
   c. She'll
   d. They've
   e. I'm
   f. We're

10. a. modal
    b. *be*
    c. *have*
    d. *be*
    e. *have*

11. a. verb
    b. aux
    c. aux
    d. verb
    e. verb

12. a. isn't
    b. hadn't
    c. won't
    d. shouldn't
    e. don't
    f. can't

13. a. 1, 16, 2, 17, 7, 9
    b. 5, 13, 15, 3
    c. 2, 17, 10, 12
    d. 6, 2, 17, 4
    e. 7, 16, 2, 17, 8, 14
    f. 11, 2, 5
    g. 13, 1, 10, 3
    h. 7, 17, 2, 13, 15, 3
    i. 16, 2, 17, 9

CHAPTER 10

Question Modalities

Exercise 23

1. List three types of questions in English, excluding echo questions.

_____________ _____________ _____________

2. Write an example of an echo yes-no question.

____

3. Change the sentences to yes-no questions.

   a. The children have been distracted all morning.

   ____

   b. Midge will be the princess in the play.

   ____

   c. The team was in Baltimore all weekend.

   ____

4. Change the sentences to yes-no questions and indicate the inversion as that of the copula verb, a *be*, *have*, or modal auxiliary.

   a. That man could be Mr. Talbot.

   ____

   b. The dog has been barking all morning.

   ____

   c. Mother is working in the garden now.

   ____

   d. The locks are rusty.

   ____

5. Identify all the transformations that would be needed to change the following to yes-no questions (specify the inversions as auxiliary or copula).

   a. The teacher arrived at 10:00.

   ____

   b. Dad has left for work.

   ____

   c. Jean may go to the pool today.

   ____

   d. A lot of sunlight damages these plants.

   ____

   e. Many people need jobs this summer.

   ____

   f. Tim was in school this morning.

   ____

6. Identify the following by matching the appropriate number(s) to each sentence.

   Modality changes: 1. negation
   2. yes-no question

   Transformations: 3. *do*-support
   4. contraction
   5. auxiliary inversion
   6. copula inversion

   a. Do some birds eat mice?

   ____

   b. Isn't Merlin clever?

   ____

   c. Doesn't that woman realize the consequences?

   ____

   d. Can the birds eat this seed?

   ____

   e. Aren't the boys in class?

   ____

Exercise 24

1. Supply the appropriate question tag for each.

   a. The artist enjoys camping in the mountains, ________________________________ ?

   b. The tourists should have arrived already, ________________________________ ?

   c. Bob can't bowl, ________________________________ ?

   d. Your aunt is a pianist, ________________________________ ?

2. Indicate if the response expected by the speaker would be *yes* or *no*.

   a. Martha didn't explain, did she? ________________________________

   b. The class cheered the performance, didn't they? ________________________________

   c. Those men can't act, can they? ________________________________

   d. Max will come to the party, won't he? ________________________________

3. Specify the modality changes and transformations required to generate the question *Mary is a doctor, isn't she?*

   ____

   ____

Exercise 25

1. Write the *wh*-word or phrase for each description.

   a. Adverbial of frequency ________________________________

   b. Noun phrase [+human] ________________________________

   c. Adverbial of time ________________________________

   d. Cardinal determiner ________________________________

   e. Adverbial of duration ________________________________

2. Identify the PRO-form that could be used for each of the *wh*-words.

   a. Who ________________________________

   b. Whose ________________________________

   c. Why ________________________________

d. How ____________________

e. When ____________________

3. Change each sentence below to a *wh*-question, using the *wh*-word for the italicized PRO-form.

a. Paul is yelling *for some reason*.

____

b. Mae will buy *something* for her friend.

____

c. *Someone* is making all that noise.

____

d. The maid cleaned *someone's* house.

____

e. The rocket will blast off *sometime*.

____

4. Identify those questions in which an auxiliary or copula inversion was needed by writing the type of inversion as *be*, *have*, *do*, modal auxiliary, or copula.

a. Who is teaching Kevin? ____________________

b. What can you eat? ____________________

c. What did the boys drink? ____________________

d. Why are we always late? ____________________

e. Where was the principal yesterday? ____________________

f. When should Charlene have finished her paper? ____________________

5. Write three echo questions using a different *wh*-word in each.

a. ____________________

b. ____________________

c. ____________________

6. Rank the *wh*-questions below in order of difficulty (using 1 for the least complex) in terms of the rules needed to formulate the questions.

   a. Where did Dad put his glasses? ______

   b. Where can the class go today? ______

   c. Why didn't the girls enjoy the play? ______

   d. Who is unhappy? ______

7. Identify the following in each sentence by matching the appropriate number(s) to the sentences.

   Modality changes:
   1. negation
   2. yes-no question
   3. *wh*-question

   Transformations:
   4. *do*-support
   5. contraction
   6. auxiliary inversion
   7. copula inversion

   a. What didn't the girls get for the picnic?

   ____

   b. Which carpenters are working on the porch?

   ____

   c. What is the committee planning for the party?

   ____

   d. Why was Dad angry?

   ____

   e. Can't you spell that word?

   ____

Exercise 23: Answers

1. yes-no questions, *wh*-questions, tag questions

2. e.g.: Your brother is working?

3. a. Have the children been distracted all morning?
   b. Will Midge be the princess in the play?
   c. Was the team in Baltimore all weekend?

4. a. Could that man be Mr. Talbot?, modal auxiliary inversion
   b. Has the dog been barking all morning?, *have* auxiliary inversion
   c. Is Mother working in the garden now?, *be* auxiliary inversion
   d. Are the locks rusty?, copula inversion

5. a. *do*-support, auxiliary inversion
   b. auxiliary inversion
   c. auxiliary inversion
   d. *do*-support, auxiliary inversion
   e. *do*-support, auxiliary inversion
   f. copula inversion

6. a. 3, 5, 2
   b. 6, 1, 4, 2
   c. 3, 5, 1, 4, 2
   d. 5, 2
   e. 6, 1, 4, 2

Exercise 24: Answers

1. a. doesn't he/she
   b. shouldn't they
   c. can he
   d. isn't she

2. a. no
   b. yes
   c. no
   d. yes

3. yes-no question, copula inversion, negation, contraction, personal pronominalization, deletion

Exercise 25: Answers

1. a. how often
   b. who
   c. when
   d. how many
   e. how long

2. a. someone
   b. someone's
   c. for some reason
   d. somehow
   e. sometime

3. a. Why is Paul yelling?
   b. What will Mae buy for her friend?
   c. Who is making all that noise?
   d. Whose house did the maid clean?
   e. When will the rocket blast off?

4. a. no auxiliary inversion
   b. modal auxiliary inversion
   c. *do* auxiliary inversion
   d. copula inversion
   e. copula inversion
   f. modal auxiliary inversion

5. a. e.g.: Tom is leaving when?
   b. e.g.: The roses bloom how often?
   c. e.g.: Dad left my money where?

6. a. 3
   b. 2
   c. 4
   d. 1

7. a. 3, 4, 6, 1, 5
   b. 3
   c. 3, 6
   d. 3, 7
   e. 2, 1, 5, 6

CHAPTER 10

Practice Test

1. List three types of questions in English, excluding echo questions.

   ______________________ ______________________ ______________________

2. Write an example of an echo yes-no question.

   ____

3. Change the sentences to yes-no questions.

   a. The teachers were busy at noon.

      ____

   b. Dean Grey has been at the college for five years.

      ____

   c. The purse could be in your locker.

      ____

4. Change the sentences to yes-no questions and indicate the inversion as the copula verb, a *be*, *have*, or modal auxiliary.

   a. Ryan should study his math.

      ____

   b. The children were watching a movie.

      ____

   c. The sky is hazy this morning.

      ____

   d. Mac has fixed the car.

      ____

5. Identify all the transformations that would be needed to change the following to yes-no questions (specify the inversion as auxiliary or copula).

   a. Mother plays the organ.

   ____

   b. Mark could have placed first in the hurdles.

   ____

   c. Bruce was a monster in the play.

   ____

   d. The girls drink iced tea for lunch.

   ____

   e. Jean made all her clothes.

   ____

6. Supply the appropriate question tag for each.

   a. Jeff was a mechanic, ______________________________?

   b. Betty can't swim, ______________________________?

   c. The teams should have left by now, ______________________________?

   d. Ted plays basketball every day, ______________________________?

7. Indicate if the response the speaker would expect would be *yes* or *no*.

   a. Carol will water the plants, won't she? ______

   b. Julian didn't lie, did he? ______

   c. The group followed the rules, didn't they? ______

   d. That man can't drive a truck, can he? ______

8. Specify the modality changes and transformations needed to generate the question *Jim can't see well, can he?*

   ____

   ____

9. Write the *wh*-word replacement for each.

   a. Cardinal determiner ____________________

   b. Noun phrase [−animate] ____________________

   c. Adverbial of duration ____________________

   d. Adverbial of place ____________________

   e. Adverbial of manner ____________________

10. Identify the PRO-form that could be used for each of the *wh*-words.

    a. How ____________________

    b. When ____________________

    c. What ____________________

    d. Why ____________________

    e. Where ____________________

11. Change each sentence below to a *wh*-question, using the *wh*-word for the italicized PRO-form.

    a. Grandmother is going *somewhere*.

    ____

    b. *Someone* is sleeping in my bed.

    ____

    c. They bought *someone's* car.

    ____

    d. Yvonne sent *something* by parcel post.

    ____

    e. Gwen is crying *for some reason*.

    ____

12. Put an X after those questions in which an auxiliary or copula inversion was needed in addition to the *wh*-modality change.

    a. Why is she at the college? ______

    b. Which groups were at the meeting? ______

    c. Where are the Cuban cigars? ______

d. When will the plane return from Boston? ______

e. Who is supervising Kitty? ______

13. Write an echo question for each of the *wh*-words.

a. What: ______

b. Where: ______

c. How many: ______

14. Identify all the complexities in each sentence by using the numbered list.

Modality changes:
1. imperative
2. negation
3. yes-no question
4. *wh*-question

Noun phrase elaborations:
5. poss determiner
6. poss noun
7. adj modifier
8. noun adjunct

Transformations:
9. pers pro
10. reflex pro
11. indef pro
12. dem pro
13. reflex pro intens
14. reflex pro intens movt
15. adv preposing
16. intensifier
17. indirect obj preposing
18. *do*-support
19. contraction
20. auxiliary inversion
21. copula inversion

a. When will Chun's plane get in? (3) ______

b. Don't the girls buy their mother gifts? (7) ______

c. Never put anything in your ear. (5) ______

d. Do those tough boys always tease your sister's dog? (7) ______

e. Why should that be so difficult for you? (5) ______

f. Every few days our neighbor gets himself in serious trouble. (4) ______

g. Who didn't do the work herself? (5) ______

h. Will he himself present the awards to the state senator? (5) ______

15. Rank the *wh*-questions below in order of difficulty (using 1 for the least complex) in terms of the rules needed to formulate the questions.

    a. Why didn't the student take the exam? _______

    b. Where did Mom hide those cookies? _______

    c. What is in your notebook? _______

    d. When will the electricians finish the work? _______

Chapter 10 Practice Test: Answers

1. yes-no questions, *wh*-questions, tag questions

2. e.g.: You are going home now?

3. a. Were the teachers busy at noon?
   b. Has Dean Grey been at the college for five years?
   c. Could the purse be in your locker?

4. a. Should Ryan study his math?, modal auxiliary inversion
   b. Were the children watching a movie?, *be* auxiliary inversion
   c. Is the sky hazy this morning?, copula inversion
   d. Has Mac fixed his car?, *have* auxiliary inversion

5. a. *do*-support, auxiliary inversion
   b. auxiliary inversion
   c. copula inversion
   d. *do*-support, auxiliary inversion
   e. *do*-support, auxiliary inversion

6. a. wasn't he
   b. can she
   c. shouldn't they
   d. doesn't he

7. a. yes
   b. no
   c. yes
   d. no

8. negation, contraction, auxiliary inversion, personal pronominalization, yes-no question, deletion

9. a. how many
   b. what
   c. how long
   d. where
   e. how

10. a. somehow
    b. sometime
    c. something
    d. for some reason
    e. somewhere

11. a. Where is Grandmother going?
    b. Who is sleeping in my bed?
    c. Whose car did they buy?
    d. What did Yvonne send by parcel post?
    e. Why is Gwen crying?

12. a, c, d

13. a. e.g.: He is bringing what to class?
    b. e.g.: Sally is going where today?
    c. e.g.: John sent how many roses?

14. a. 4, 20, 6
    b. 3, 18, 20, 2, 19, 17, 5
    c. 2, 1, 15, 11, 5
    d. 18, 20, 3, 7, 15, 5, 6
    e. 4, 20, 12, 16, 9
    f. 15, 5, 10, 7
    g. 4, 18, 2, 19, 14
    h. 3, 20, 9, 13, 8

15. a. 4
    b. 3
    c. 1
    d. 2

CHAPTER 11

Particle Movement and *There* Transformation

Exercise 26

1. Put an X after those sentences that contain a particle movement.

   a. The officer looked the crowd over quickly. ______

   b. Casey threw the bat over the umpire's head. ______

   c. The boy walked the dogs up the hill ______

   d. We'll cut the pumpkin up tomorrow. ______

   e. How could these men hold the bank up so easily? ______

2. What is the feature of the verb + prt needed for the particle movement?

   ____

3. State a condition under which the particle movement is obligatory.

   ____

4. Indicate whether the italicized word is a preposition (prep) or particle (prt).

   a. The teacher checked *over* the papers. ______

   b. Jack was counting *on* that bonus. ______

   c. The bird carried *away* the worm. ______

   d. We drove *over* the bridge. ______

   e. Japanese children count *on* an abacus. ______

5. Put an X after those sentences that could be rewritten with particle movement.

   a. An old friend called up yesterday. ______

   b. Selma cleared off the table. ______

   c. The child ran away from home. ______

d. Jean called up her friends. _______

e. The waitress set down the pitcher. _______

Exercise 27

1. State two conditions under which the *there* transformation is applicable.

   a. ____

   b. ____

2. Put an X after those sentences that can be transformed using *there*.

   a. Three dining room chairs may be in the attic. _______

   b. Sheila is in South Carolina. _______

   c. A better pen should be in the top drawer. _______

   d. Everyone was sitting on the floor. _______

   e. Only one child is in the pool right now. _______

3. Write adv preposing (AP) after those sentences in which you do not have a *there* transformation.

   a. There are several stuffed cabbages on the table. _______

   b. There his glasses are on the dashboard. _______

   c. There the dictionary is near the shelf. _______

   d. There was lint on the sweater. _______

   e. There is much noise in the nursery. _______

4. When appropriate, identify the following transformations in the sentences.

   1. adverbial preposing
   2. particle movement
   3. there

   a. There your sweater is. _______

   b. Everywhere there were trees along the road. _______

   c. You should put your books away. _______

   d. At two o'clock they put the cat out. _______

   e. There wasn't anyone there. _______

Exercise 26: Answers

1. a, d, e

2. [+transitive]

3. The particle movement is obligatory when NP^2 is a personal, reflexive, or demonstrative pronoun.

4. a. prt
   b. prt
   c. prt
   d. prep
   e. prep

5. b, d, e

Exercise 27: Answers

1. a. The noun phrase (NP^1) has a −definite determiner.
   b. The verb phrase contains a *be* + adverbial.

2. a, c, e

3. b, c

4. a. 1
   b. 1, 3
   c. 2
   d. 1, 2
   e. 3

CHAPTER 11

Practice Test

1. Put an X after those sentences that contain a particle movement.

   a. When did you last clean your room up? _______

   b. They wiped the sweat off their foreheads. _______

   c. Did they really burn the house down themselves? _______

   d. He kept the library books over the holidays. _______

   e. The coach lined his players up on the field. _______

2. What is the feature of the verb + prt needed for the particle movement?

   ____

3. State a condition under which the particle movement is obligatory.

   ____

4. Indicate whether the italicized word is a preposition (prep) or particle (prt).

   a. We kept *up* the good work. _______

   b. Stan headed *up* the road. _______

   c. Ellen brought *in* the newspaper. _______

   d. The dog ran *out of* the yard. _______

   e. Edward looked *in* the box. _______

5. Indicate with an X those sentences in which particle movement would be possible.

   a. Gary set down the wood. _______

   b. The power went out with no warning. _______

   c. The apples turned to gold. _______

   d. Grandma called up this morning. _______

   e. We cleaned out the basement. _______

6. Indicate all the modality changes, noun phrase elaborations, and transformations in the sentences by using the numbered list.

Modality changes:	1. imperative
	2. negation
	3. yes-no question
	4. *wh*-question
Noun Phrase Elaborations:	5. poss determiner
	6. poss noun
	7. adj modifier
	8. noun adjunct
Transformations:	9. pers pro
	10. reflex pro
	11. indef pro
	12. dem pro
	13. reflex pro intens
	14. reflex pro intens movt
	15. adv preposing
	16. intensifier
	17. indirect obj preposing
	18. *do*-support
	19. contraction
	20. aux invers
	21. copula invers
	22. particle movement
	23. there

a. Why isn't there a woman in the position? (5) ______________________

b. John himself sent the memo out to his clients. (3) ______________________

c. Is Dad getting her a dog for Christmas? (4) ______________________

d. Always leave the baby's carriage under a shade tree. (4) ______________________

e. Didn't someone pick that up this morning? (8) ______________________

f. Aren't there any tools in the small shed? (6) ______________________

g. How did your brother put these shelves up himself? (6) ______________________

h. Who is showing the children those monster films? (3) ______________________

7. State two conditions under which the *there* transformation is applicable.

   a. ______________________________

   b. ______________________________

8. Put an X after those sentences that can be transformed using *there*.

   a. Several birds are in the birdhouse. _______

   b. Two hangers were in that closet. _______

   c. Even more guests are in the garden. _______

   d. My aunt is in the dining room. _______

   e. Those boys were in the gymnasium. _______

9. Write adverbial preposing (AP) by those sentences in which you do not have a *there* transformation.

   a. There are some flowers in the basket. ______________________________

   b. There was a baby chick in the box. ______________________________

   c. There are many teams in the tournament. ______________________________

   d. There my shoes are under the couch. ______________________________

   e. There the address is on that slip of paper. ______________________________

Chapter 11 Practice Test: Answers

1. a, c, e

2. [+transitive]

3. The particle movement is obligatory when the NP^2 is a personal, reflexive, or demonstrative pronoun.

4. a. prt
   b. prep
   c. prt
   d. prep
   e. prep

5. a, e

6. a. 4, 21, 2, 19, 23
   b. 13, 22, 5
   c. 3, 20, 9, 17
   d. 15, 1, 6, 8
   e. 3, 18, 20, 2, 19, 11, 12, 22
   f. 3, 21, 2, 19, 23, 7
   g. 4, 18, 20, 5, 22, 14
   h. 4, 17, 8

7. a. the noun phrase (NP^1) has a −definite determiner
   b. the verb phrase contains a *be* + adverbial

8. a, b, c

9. d, e

CHAPTER 12
The Passive Transformation

Exercise 28

1. What feature must verbs carry to have passive voice?

____

2. Write the tense and voice for each of the verb phrases.

	Tense	*Voice*
a. will be exercising	____________	____________
b. were delayed	____________	____________
c. could be reached	____________	____________
d. has been delivered	____________	____________
e. had sewn	____________	____________

3. Identify each passive sentence as reversible (R) or nonreversible (NR).

   a. The child was struck by a teacher. ______

   b. The birds' nests were damaged by the storm. ______

   c. The oceanliner was sunk by a mine. ______

   d. The prisoners were beaten by the guards. ______

   e. The package was delivered by the mail carrier. ______

4. Write the active sentence for each of the following.

   a. The report is being typed by the secretary.

   ____

   b. The vase was broken by the child.

   ____

   c. The copper tubing should be installed by the plumber.

   ____

d. A different site had been suggested by the major.

____

e. The horse may be shot by the owner.

____

5. Indicate with a sentence the information that could be received by a person who used a surface order strategy.

   a. The car was destroyed by the van.

   ____

   b. The teacher was robbed by the student.

   ____

Exercise 29

1. What is deleted in truncated passive sentences?

____

2. State a condition under which the truncated passive would be used.

____

3. Identify each sentence as truncated (T) or nontruncated (NT) and as reversible (R) or nonreversible (NR).

   a. A poll must be taken by the network. _____ _____

   b. Bonnie was picked up by a friend. _____ _____

   c. The paper was written by midnight. _____ _____

   d. The Mets were defeated by the eighth inning. _____ _____

   e. The baby carriage had been left by the front door. _____ _____

4. Write a truncated passive sentence for each of the following.

   a. Someone should have filled out the forms.

   ____

   b. Somebody must spray the fern.

   ____

c. Someone is painting our car.

____

5. Identify the tense and voice of each of the italicized verb phrases.

The classroom teachers (a) *had been encouraged* to attend the discussion on mainstreaming. Many topics (b) *were discussed*. Several teachers (c) *had worried* about calling on hearing-impaired students. We reminded them that if hearing-impaired students (d) *had been placed* in their classes, then, they should be able to participate in all the work. Other areas of concern (e) *were brought up*, so that another meeting (f) *has been scheduled* for next week.

	Tense	*Voice*
a.	______________	______________
b.	______________	______________
c.	______________	______________
d.	______________	______________
e.	______________	______________
f.	______________	______________

6. Identify those sentences that are passive with or without deletion by writing in the blank (pass), or (pass) and (del).

   a. When had the letter been mailed? __________

   b. Was the food eaten by 2:00? __________

   c. Harold should have been informed. __________

   d. The children have been quiet all morning. __________

   e. Regina was struck by lightning. __________

   f. Are they all being investigated by the IRS? __________

   g. All the pipes were drained. __________

   h. Our roof could have been badly damaged. __________

Exercise 28: Answers

1. [+transitive]

2. a. present, active
   b. past, passive
   c. past, passive
   d. present, passive
   e. past, active

3. a. R
   b. NR
   c. NR
   d. R
   e. NR

4. a. The secretary is typing the report.
   b. The child broke the vase.
   c. The plumber should install the copper tubing.
   d. The major had suggested a different site.
   e. The owner may shoot the horse.

5. a. The car destroyed the van.
   b. The teacher robbed the student.

Exercise 29: Answers

1. The *by* + agent (or NP^1)

2. When the agent or NP^1 is unknown or unimportant

3. a. NT, NR
   b. NT, R
   c. T, NR
   d. T, R
   e. T, NR

4. a. The forms should have been filled out.
   b. The fern must be sprayed.
   c. Our car is being painted.

5. a. past, passive
   b. past, passive
   c. past, active
   d. past, passive
   e. past, passive
   f. present, passive

6. a. pass, del
   b. pass, del
   c. pass, del
   d. (no passive)
   e. pass
   f. pass
   g. pass, del
   h. pass, del

CHAPTER 12

Practice Test

1. What feature must verbs carry to have passive voice?

____

2. Write the tense and voice for each of the verb phrases.

	Tense	*Voice*
a. was arrested	____________	____________
b. were broken	____________	____________
c. has been elected	____________	____________
d. should be staying	____________	____________
e. may be burned	____________	____________

3. Identify each passive sentence as reversible (R) or nonreversible (NR).

   a. The car was driven by a stunt man. ______

   b. The van was hit by a dump truck. ______

   c. The puppy was groomed by an expert. ______

   d. The dog was killed by a car. ______

   e. The couple was followed by the robber. ______

4. Write the active sentence for each of the following.

   a. The party may be catered by Marriott.

   ____

   b. A ticket had been given to the driver by the police officer.

   ____

   c. The stereo could be repaired by my friend.

   ____

d. The plane was flown by a skilled pilot.

____

e. The operation is being performed by a famous surgeon.

____

5. Indicate with a sentence the information that could be received by a person who used a surface-reading-order strategy.

   a. The antelope was injured by the tiger.

   ____

   b. The lawyer was robbed by the woman.

   ____

6. What is deleted in truncated passive sentences?

   ____

7. State a condition under which the truncated passive would be used.

   ____

8. Identify each sentence as truncated (T) or nontruncated (NT) and as reversible (R) or nonreversible (NR).

   a. The new pilot was helped out by an instructor.

   __________ __________

   b. The election was won by a landslide.

   __________ __________

   c. Tommy got stung by bees.

   __________ __________

   d. A chairperson must be appointed by the committee.

   __________ __________

   e. The books had been placed on the shelves.

   __________ __________

9. Identify all the complexities in each sentence by using the numbered list.

Modality changes:	1. imperative	3. yes-no question
	2. negation	4. *wh*-question
Noun phrase elaborations:	5. poss determiner	7. adj modifier
	6. poss noun	8. noun adjunct
Transformations:	9. pers pro	18. *do*-support
	10. reflex pro	19. contraction
	11. indef pro	20. aux invers
	12. dem pro	21. copula invers
	13. reflex pro intens	22. prt movt
	14. reflex pro intens movt	23. there
	15. adv preposing	24. passive
	16. intensifier	25. deletion
	17. indirect obj preposing	

a. When did Dad send Mary a check for Tom's gift? (5)

____

b. Shouldn't the TV have been turned off during our spring vacation? (8)

____

c. Yesterday all their clothes were left out in the rain. (4)

____

d. She wasn't disturbed by that loud noise. (5)

____

e. Before noon, take the dog out for a short walk. (4)

____

f. Why can't they be married in December? (7)

____

g. Are Helen's children always so shy in nursery school? (6)

____

h. The pilots themselves were disturbed by the extremely warm temperatures. (4)

____

i. Will everybody be inoculated? (5)

____

10. Write a truncated passive sentence for each of the following.

    a. Somebody should clean the room.

    ____

    b. Someone must have taken out the trash.

    ____

    c. Something damaged the finish on this table.

    ____

11. Identify the tense and voice of each of the italicized verb phrases.

    The mainstreaming program (a) *was started* last fall. Classroom teachers (b) *were counseled* about special needs of the hearing-impaired child. They (c) *had seen* an informative film after which many questions (d) *had been answered*. Weekly report forms (e) *were given* to each teacher. We (f) *had expected* some objection about these forms, but did not receive any.

	Tense	*Voice*
a.	____________	____________
b.	____________	____________
c.	____________	____________
d.	____________	____________
e.	____________	____________
f.	____________	____________

Chapter 12 Practice Test: Answers

1. [+ transitive]

2. a. past, passive
   b. past, passive
   c. present, passive
   d. past, active
   e. present, passive

3. a. NR
   b. R
   c. NR
   d. NR
   e. R

4. a. Marriott may cater the party.
   b. The police officer had given a ticket to the driver.
   c. My friend could repair the stereo.
   d. A skilled pilot flew the plane.
   e. A famous surgeon is performing the operation.

5. a. The antelope injured the tiger.
   b. The lawyer robbed the woman.

6. *by* + the agent or NP[1]

7. When the NP in the active sentence is unknown or unimportant.

8. a. NT, R
   b. T, NR
   c. NT, NR
   d. NT, R
   e. T, NR

9. a. 4, 18, 20, 17, 6
   b. 3, 20, 2, 19, 24, 25, 5, 8
   c. 15, 5, 24, 25
   d. 9, 2, 19, 24, 7
   e. 15, 1, 22, 7
   f. 4, 20, 2, 19, 9, 24, 25
   g. 3, 21, 6, 15, 16, 8
   h. 13, 24, 16, 7
   i. 3, 20, 11, 24, 25

10. a. The room should be cleaned.
    b. The trash must have been taken out.
    c. The finish on this table was damaged.

11. a. past, passive
    b. past, passive
    c. past, active
    d. past, passive
    e. past, passive
    f. past, active

CHAPTER 13

Language Analysis II Exercise

Complete both syntactic and semantic descriptions and summaries for the following hypothetical sample. Use the sample in chapter 13 as a guide.

Language Sample

1. You're not the winner.
2. Which book does Dad have?
3. That tree was knocked down last night.
4. There was a big elephant at the zoo.
5. Susie handed the elephant a peanut.
6. Bite her hand off.
7. Yesterday she was sewing.
8. Why is Tom so ugly?
9. Did he polish the wood floors with a cloth?
10. The baby likes anything.
11. She hasn't cried for two hours.
12. Could they sleep on Mary's sofa bed?

Syntactic Description

1. You're not the winner.

   VP modulation:

   NP modulation:

   Modality change:

   Transformation:

2. Which book does Dad have?

VP modulation:

NP modulation:

Modality change:

Transformation:

3. That tree was knocked down last night.

VP modulation:

NP modulation:

Transformation:

4. There was a big elephant at the zoo.

VP modulation:

NP modulation:

NP elaboration:

Transformation:

5. Susie handed the elephant a peanut.

   VP modulation:

   NP modulation:

   Transformation:

6. Bite her hand off.

   VP modulation:

   NP elaboration:

   Modality change:

   Transformation:

7. Yesterday she was sewing.

   VP modulation:

   Transformation:

8. Why is Tom so ugly?

   VP modulation:

   NP modulation:

Modality change:

Transformation:

9. Did he polish the wood floors with a cloth?

VP modulation:

NP modulation:

NP elaboration:

Modality change:

Transformation:

10. The baby likes anything.

VP modulation:

NP modulation:

Transformation:

11. She hasn't cried for two hours.

VP modulation:

NP modulation:

Modality change:

Transformation:

12. Could they sleep on Mary's sofa bed?

    VP modulation:

    NP modulation:

    NP elaboration:

    Modality change:

    Transformation:

Syntactic Summary

Sentences	*Frequency of Occurrence*	*Comments*
Pattern 1	______	______
Pattern 2	______	______
Pattern 3	______	______
Pattern 4	______	______
Pattern 5	______	______

Verb Phrase Modulations

regular past	______	______
regular 3rd person	______	______
modal	______	______
copula	______	______
be auxiliary	______	______
progressive	______	______
perfect	______	______
preposition	______	______
particle	______	______
have aux	______	______

Noun Phrase Modulations	*Frequency of Occurrence*	*Comments*
regular plural	________	________
articles	________	________
demonstratives	________	________
cardinals	________	________
ordinals	________	________
Noun Phrase Elaborations		
possessive determiner	________	________
possessive noun	________	________
adjective	________	________
noun adjunct	________	________
Modality Changes		
negation	________	________
imperative	________	________
yes-no question	________	________
wh-question	________	________
Transformations		
pronominalization:		
personal	________	________
indefinite	________	________
do-support	________	________
auxiliary or copula inversion	________	________
contraction	________	________
adverbial preposing	________	________
intensifier	________	________
indirect object preposing	________	________
particle movement	________	________
there	________	________
passive	________	________
deletion	________	________

Semantic Description

1. You're not the winner.

2. Which book does Dad have?

3. That tree was knocked down last night.

4. There was a big elephant at the zoo.

5. Susie handed the elephant a peanut.

6. Bite her hand off.

7. Yesterday she was sewing.

8. Why is Tom so ugly?

9. Did he polish the wood floors with a cloth?

10. The baby likes anything.

11. She hasn't cried for two hours.

12. Could they sleep on Mary's sofa bed?

Semantic Summary

Number of utterances:

Number of propositions:

Number of propositions per utterance:

	Frequency of Occurrence
Noun cases	
Mover	______
Agent	______
Experiencer	______
Patient	______
Entity	______
Equivalent	______
Beneficiary	______
Possessor	______
Part	______
Verb cases	
Action	______
Process	______
Stative	______
Modifier cases	
Condition	______
Size	______
Cardinal	______
Ordinal	______
Adverbial cases	
Location	______
Time	______
Duration	______
Reason	______
Instrument	______
Intensifier	______

Language Analysis II Exercise: Answers

Syntactic Description

1. You're not the winner. $NP^1 + V_L + NP^1$

VP modulation:	contracted copula
NP modulation:	+def art
Modality change:	negation
Transformation:	contraction
	personal pronominalization

2. Which book does Dad have?
   Dad has some book. $NP^1 + V + NP^2$
   VP modulation: (*do* aux)
   NP modulation: Ø art
   Modality change: *wh*-question
   Transformation: auxiliary inversion
   do-support

3. That tree was knocked down last night.
   (Someone) knocked down that tree last night. $NP^1 + V + NP^2 + Adv$
   VP modulation: (*be* aux)
   particle
   NP modulation: demonstrative
   ordinal
   Transformation: passive
   deletion

4. There was a big elephant at the zoo.
   A big elephant was at the zoo. $NP + V_{be} + Adv$
   VP modulation: uncontracted copula
   preposition
   NP modulation: −def art
   +def art
   NP elaboration: adjective modifier
   Transformation: there

5. Susie handed the elephant a peanut.
   Susie handed a peanut to the elephant. $NP^1 + V + NP^2 + Adv$
   VP modulation: regular past
   NP modulation: Ø article
   −def art
   +def art
   Transformation: indirect object preposing

6. Bite her hand off.
   (You) bite off her hand. $(NP^1) + V + NP^2$
   VP modulation: particle
   NP elaboration: possessive determiner
   Modality change: imperative
   Transformation: particle movement

7. Yesterday she was sewing.
   She was sewing yesterday. $NP + V_i + Adv$
   VP modulation: *be* aux
   progressive
   Transformation: personal pronominalization
   adverbial preposing

8. Why is Tom so ugly?
   Tom is ugly (for some reason). $NP + V_L + Adj + Adv$
   VP modulation: uncontracted copula
   NP modulation: Ø art
   Modality change: *wh*-question
   Transformation: copula inversion
   intensifier

9. Did he polish the wood floors with a cloth? $NP^1 + V + NP^2 + Adv$
   He polished the wood floors with a cloth.
   VP modulation: (*do* aux)
   preposition (*with*)
   NP modulation: +def art
   −def art
   regular plural
   NP elaboration: noun adjunct
   Modality change: yes-no question
   Transformation: *do*-support
   auxiliary inversion
   personal pronominalization

10. The baby likes anything. $NP^1 + V + NP^2$
   VP modulation: regular 3rd person
   NP modulation: +def art
   Transformation: indefinite pronominalization

11. She hasn't cried for two hours. $NP + V_i + Adv$
   VP modulation: *have* aux
   perfect aspect
   preposition (*for*)
   NP modulation: cardinal
   reg plural
   Modality change: negation
   Transformation: personal pronominalization
   contraction

12. Could they sleep on Mary's sofa bed? $NP + V_i + Adv$
   VP modulation: modal aux
   preposition (*on*)
   NP modulation: Ø art
   NP elaboration: possessive noun
   noun adjunct
   Modality change: yes-no question
   Transformation: personal pronominalization
   auxiliary inversion

Syntactic Summary

Sentences	*Frequency of Occurrence*	*Comments*
Pattern 1	3	adverbials (3)
Pattern 2	6	adverbials (1)
Pattern 3	1	
Pattern 4	1	
Pattern 5	1	

	Frequency of Occurrence	Comments
Verb Phrase Modulations		
regular past	1	
regular 3rd person	1	
modal	1	could
copula	3	
be aux	2	1 contracted, 1 in passive
progressive	1	
perfect	1	
preposition	4	has + neg contraction
particle	2	at, for, on, with
have aux	1	
Noun Phrase Modulation		
regular plural	2	
articles	12	a, the, Ø
demonstratives	1	that
cardinals	1	two
ordinals	1	last
Noun Phrase Elaborations		
possessive determiner	1	
possessive noun	1	her
adjective	1	
noun adjunct	2	
Modality Changes		
negation	2	not, contraction
imperative	1	
yes-no question	2	did, could
wh-question	2	reason – why which + N
Transformations		
pronominalization:		
personal	5	you, she, he, they
indefinite	1	anything
do-support	2	does, did
auxiliary or copula inversion	4	
contraction	2	copula + pronoun, neg contraction + *have* aux
adverbial preposing	1	time
intensifier	1	so
indirect object preposing	1	
particle movement	1	
there	1	
passive	1	truncated
deletion	1	

Semantic Description

1. You're not the winner.	Entity—stative—equivalent
2. Which book does Dad have?	
Dad have book	Possessor—process—patient
3. That tree was knocked down last night.	
someone knock down tree night	Agent—action—patient—ordinal—time
4. There was a big elephant at the zoo.	
elephant be (at) zoo	Entity—stative—location
elephant be big	Entity—stative—size
5. Susie handed a peanut to the elephant.	Agent—action—patient—beneficiary
6. Bite her hand off.	
someone bite off hand	Agent—action—patient
someone have hand	Entity—stative—part
7. Yesterday she was sewing.	
someone sew yesterday	Mover—action—time
8. Why is Tom so ugly?	
Tom be ugly (for some reason)	Entity—stative—intensifier—quality—reason
9. Did he polish the wood floors with a cloth?	
someone polish floor (with) cloth	Agent—action—patient—instrument
floor be wood	Entity—stative—equivalent
10. The baby likes anything.	Experiencer—process—patient
11. She hasn't cried for two hours.	Mover—action—cardinal—duration
12. Could they sleep on Mary's sofa bed?	
someone sleep (on) bed	Experiencer—process—location
Mary have bed	Possessor—process—patient
bed be sofa	Entity—stative—equivalent

Semantic Summary

Number of utterances:	12
Number of propositions:	17
Number of propositions per utterance:	1.4

	Frequency of Occurrence
Noun cases	
Mover	2
Agent	4
Experiencer	2
Patient	7
Entity	7
Equivalent	3
Beneficiary	1
Possessor	2
Part	1
Verb cases	
Action	6
Process	4
Stative	7
Modifier cases	
Quality	1
Size	1
Cardinal	1
Ordinal	1
Adverbial cases	
Location	2
Time	2
Duration	1
Reason	1
Instrument	1
Intensifier	1

CHAPTERS 1–13

Review Test

1. Write the appropriate word(s) for each.

   a. first person singular reflexive ____________________

   b. third person plural accusative personal pronoun ____________________

   c. second person plural reflexive ____________________

   d. modal negative contraction ____________________

   e. indefinite pronoun with a negative morpheme ____________________

   f. intransitive verb plus adverbial ____________________

   g. first person singular present copula ____________________

   h. first person singular genitive personal pronoun ____________________

   i. regular past of a process verb ____________________

   j. regular third singular of an action verb ____________________

2. Identify each passive transformation as reversible (R) or nonreversible (NR) and as truncated (T) or non-truncated (NT).

   a. The pilot was killed by the hijacker. ____________________

   b. Ms. Smith could have been duped by a friend. ____________________

   c. The fire was put out with a small extinguisher. ____________________

   d. The issue is being considered by the committee now. ____________________

3. a. Write the active sentence for (2b).

   ____

   b. Write the active sentence for (2c).

   ____

   c. Write the proposition(s) and semantic relationship(s) expressed in (2a).

   ____

   d. Write the proposition(s) and semantic relationship(s) expressed in (2d).

   ____

4. Identify all the complexities in each sentence using the numbered list.

Modality changes:	1. negation	
	2. imperative	
	3. yes-no question	
	4. *wh*-question	
Noun phrase elaborations:	5. poss determiner	
	6. poss noun	
	7. adjective	
	8. noun adjunct	
Transformations:	9. pers pro	18. *do*-support
	10. reflex pro	19. contraction
	11. indef pro	20. aux inversion
	12. dem pro	21. copula inversion
	13. reflex pro intens	22. prt movt
	14. reflex pro intens movt	23. there
	15. adv preposing	24. passive
	16. intensifier	25. deletion
	17. indirect obj preposing	

a. Every Sunday the clock should be wound. (3) ________________

b. Will Dr. May herself call me? (4) ________________

c. Don't cut yourself with that sharp knife. (6) ________________

d. Tonight there's a really good movie on Channel 5. (5) ________________

e. Did Brad tell the teacher a lie about his brother? (5) ________________

f. Why doesn't Sally knit herself a nylon sweater? (8) ________________

g. Can some stories be told many times? (4) ________________

h. Is that shirt big enough for you? (4) ________________

i. In the morning there'll be no one on that lovely beach. (6) ________________

j. When was that large tree cut down? (5) ________________

k. He was struck by lightning on the golf course. (3) ________________

l. How often can Tom's brother take the dog out for us? (5) ________________

5. Read the paragraph and fill in the blanks *a* through *m*.

(S1) Sue and Blake had arrived at the airport at noon. (S2) At 12:30 p.m. their *bags* were loaded in the trunk, and they were on their way home. (S3) *Suddenly* the car was struck from behind. (S4) Gas was spilling all over the road. (S5) Blake stopped the car, and everyone ran. (S6) The *driver* of the other car had turned his motor off, and he was lying over the steering wheel.

a. the tense and aspect of the VP in S1

____

b. the type of adverbial(s) in S1

____

c. three transformations in the first clause in S2 (up to the comma)

____

d. the tense and voice of the first VP in S2

____

e. the personal pronoun in S2 and its referent

____

f. the features of the italicized noun in S2

[count] [common] [concrete] [singular]

g. the tense and voice of the VP in S3

____

h. the transformation in S3 illustrated by the italicized word

____

i. the tense and aspect of the VP in S4

____

j. the type of pronominalization in S5

____

k. the tense and voice of the first VP in S6

____

l. the pronominalization in S6 (forward, backward)

____

m. the features of the italicized noun in S6

[human] [count] [common] [singular]

6. Label each italicized word with the correct number.

1. intensifier
2. adverb
3. pronoun
4. determiner
5. adjective
6. preposition
7. particle

a. *about* ten o'clock ____________

b. come *into* the water ____________

c. mull *over* the problem ____________

d. *really* ill ____________

e. *cooly* solved the problem ____________

f. for *everyone* ____________

g. *their* books ____________

h. in *cool* water ____________

i. *for* ten dollars ____________

j. *every* day ____________

k. walked *through* the hall ____________

l. for *them* ____________

m. *too* slowly ____________

n. push the tree *over* ____________

7. Complete a syntactic description for each of the following. Include sentence pattern, NP and VP rules, NP elaborations, modality changes, and transformations.

   a. When did Mother get that good idea?

      pattern:

      VP modulation:

      NP modulation:

      NP elaboration:

      Modality change:

      Transformation:

   b. Was that turkey big enough?

      pattern:

      VP modulation:

      NP modulation:

      Modality change:

      Transformation:

c. Pass Florence the cranberries.

pattern:

NP modulation:

Modality change:

Transformation:

d. Pam's making a new dress for Thanksgiving.

pattern:

VP modulation:

NP modulation:

NP elaboration:

Transformation:

e. All of the grades must be turned in by Wednesday.

pattern:

VP modulation:

NP modulation:

Transformation:

f. Gerald's little brother cannot spell.

pattern:

VP modulation:

NP modulation:

NP elaboration:

Modality change:

8. Complete a semantic description for each of the sentences in 7.

a. ______________________________

____

b. ______________________________

c. ______________________________

d. ______________________________

____

e. ______________________________

f. ______________________________

____

____

Chapters 1–13 Review Test: Answers

1. a. myself
   b. them
   c. yourselves
   d. won't (wouldn't, can't, etc.)
   e. nothing (no one, nobody)
   f. e.g.: go home, walk to work, etc.
   g. am
   h. mine
   i. e.g.: dissolved, wondered, etc.
   j. e.g.: runs, sews, etc.

2. a. R, NT
   b. R, NT
   c. NR, T
   d. NR, NT

3. a. A friend could have duped Ms. Smith.
   b. Someone put out the fire with a small extinguisher.
   c. The hijacker killed the pilot:
      Agent—action—patient
   d. The committee is considering the issue now:
      Experiencer—process—complement—time

4. a. 15, 24, 25
   b. 3, 20, 13, 9
   c. 2, 18, 1, 19, 10, 7
   d. 15, 23, 19, 16, 7
   e. 3, 18, 20, 17, 5
   f. 4, 18, 20, 1, 19, 17, 10, 8
   g. 3, 20, 24, 25
   h. 3, 21, 16, 9
   i. 15, 23, 19, 1, 11, 7
   j. 4, 20, 7, 24, 25
   k. 9, 24, 8
   l. 4, 20, 6, 22, 9

5. a. past, perfect
   b. location, time
   c. adv preposing, passive, deletion
   d. past, passive
   e. they, Sue and Blake
   f. [+count], [+common], [+concrete], [−singular]
   g. past passive
   h. adv preposing
   i. past, progressive
   j. indefinite pro
   k. past, active
   l. forward
   m. [+human], [+count], [+common], [+singular]

6. a. 6
   b. 6
   c. 7
   d. 1
   e. 2
   f. 3
   g. 4
   h. 5
   i. 6
   j. 4
   k. 6
   l. 3
   m. 1
   n. 7

7. a. When did Mother get that good idea?
   Mother got that good idea sometime.
   pattern: NP¹ + V + NP² + Adv
   VP modulation: (*do* aux)
   NP modulation: Ø art
   demonstrative
   NP elaboration: adjective
   Modality change: *wh*-question
   Transformation: *do*-support
   auxiliary inversion

   b. Was that turkey big enough?
   That turkey was big enough.
   pattern: NP + V_L + Adj
   VP modulation: uncontracted copula
   NP modulation: demonstrative
   Modality change: yes-no question
   Transformation: copula inversion
   intensifier

   c. Pass Florence the cranberries.
   (You) pass the cranberries to Florence.
   pattern: (NP¹ + V + NP² + Adv
   NP modulation: +def art
   Ø art
   reg plural
   Modality change: imperative
   Transformation: indirect object preposing

   d. Pam's making a new dress for Thanksgiving.
   pattern: NP¹ + V + NP² + Adv
   VP modulation: *be* aux
   progressive
   prep (for)
   NP modulation: Ø art (2)
   −def art
   NP elaboration: adjective
   Transformation: contraction

   e. All of the grades must be turned in by Wednesday.
   (The teachers) must turn in all of the grades by Wednesday.
   pattern: NP¹ + V + NP² + Adv
   VP modulation: (*be* aux)
   modal aux
   prep (by)
   particle
   NP modulation: preart
   +def art
   Ø art
   reg plural
   Transformation: passive
   deletion

   f. Gerald's little brother cannot spell.
   pattern: NP + V_i
   VP modulation: modal aux
   NP modulation: Ø art
   NP elaboration: poss noun
   adjective
   Modality change: negation

8. a. Experiencer—process—complement—time,
   Entity—stative—quality
   b. Entity—stative—size—intensifier
   c. Agent—action—patient—beneficiary
   d. Agent—action—complement—reason,
   Entity—stative—age
   e. Agent—action—patient—time
   f. Experiencer—process (brother—spell),
   Possessor—process—patient (Gerald have brother),
   Entity—stative—size (brother be little)

CHAPTER 14

Coordination

Exercise 30

1. List three operations used to expand utterances by combining two or more propositions in a single sentence.

   ________________ ________________ ________________

2. List three coordinating conjunctions.

   ________________ ________________ ________________

3. Define

   a. clause: ________________________________

   ____

   b. independent clause: ________________________________

   ____

4. State a condition that must exist if sentences are conjoined with *and*.

   ____

   ____

5. Conjoin the following pairs of sentences using personal pronouns in the second clause for the identical noun phrase(s) in the sentences.

   a. Kittie washed the clothes.
   Kittie hung up the clothes outside.

   ____

   b. Sal bought a new car.
   Sal drove the new car home.

   ____

   c. My mother gave the crystal to Ann.
   Ann washed the crystal.

   ____

d. Dad fixed the chair for Mother.
Mother put the chair in the living room.

____

6. State a condition under which identical elements may be deleted in conjoinings.

____

____

7. Identify the conjoined constituents as subjects (S), verbs (V), direct objects (DO), adjectives (Adj), adverbials (Adv), indirect objects (IO), or predicate nominatives (PN).

   a. The ants climbed over the tablecloth and onto the food. _______

   b. Marsha despises basketball and hockey. _______

   c. His manner was stern and puzzling. _______

   d. The inmates protested and booed at the meeting. _______

   e. Mustard and mayonnaise are good on sandwiches. _______

   f. My cousin sent invitations to Charles and Tim. _______

   g. Bob is a physicist and a chemist. _______

8. Write the sentences from which each sentence was derived.

   a. Marvin walked south and Bill east.

   ____

   ____

   b. They displayed their pottery and paintings.

   ____

   ____

9. List three words that may require a conjoined noun phrase in a sentence that would not be derived from two sentences. Write a sentence with a conjoined NP for each word.

   a. ______________ : ______________________________

   b. ______________ : ______________________________

   c. ______________ : ______________________________

10. Rank the sentences (using 1 for the easiest) according to their possible syntactic difficulty for children with language problems.

    a. The alarm sounded, and the fire fighters came. __________

    b. Joe found a beautiful apartment, and he rented it. __________

    c. The judge sentenced the woman, and she cried. __________

11. State two conditions under which sentences may be conjoined with *but*.

    a. __________

    b. __________

12. Indicate in the blank at the right whether the sentences would be more appropriately conjoined with *and* or *but*.

    a. The tourists went to the White House.
       They saw the president. __________

    b. John is an atheist.
       He goes to church every Sunday. __________

    c. Abe went to the mountains.
       He didn't go hiking. __________

    d. She crocheted an afghan.
       She later sold it. __________

13. What is an alternative conjunction that could substitute for *but*?

    ____

14. State a condition necessary for sentences to be conjoined with *or*.

    ____

15. State the obligatory modality change that must be present in the first of two sentences joined with *nor*.

    ____

16. When conjoining sentences such as *Jane didn't clean the house* and *Jane didn't wash the clothes*, use *nor* and keep the auxiliary in the verb phrase. Name two changes that must be made in the second sentence.

    a. __________

    b. __________

17. Identify the coordination as conjunction (C), disjunction (D), or alternation (A).

    a. Tony laughed at the joke, but he didn't think it was funny. ______________

    b. Dad washed the car and drove it into the garage. ______________

    c. You may leave on Wednesday or stay all week. ______________

    d. Estelle did no homework, nor did she clean her room. ______________

    e. The group visited only England, France, and Germany. ______________

18. Conjoin the sets of sentences using the most appropriate conjunction—*but*, *or*, *nor*, or *and*. Use each conjunction listed.

    a. You may wait here.
       You may wait in the secretary's office.

       ____

    b. Cecilia can't whistle.
       She can't hum a tune. (retain *she*)

       ____

    c. I must go.
       I'll start to cry.

       ____

    d. Close the door.
       Turn off the lights.

       ____

    e. Myron was articulate.
       He became speechless in class.

       ____

19. Write all the exact words that were deleted.

    a. Myra bought some milk, flour, and sugar.

       ____

    b. Felix wants to swim but can't.

       ____

    c. Sue and Jason cleaned the yard.

       ____

Exercise 31

1. List three pairs of correlative conjunctions.

_______________ _______________ _______________

2. Identify the conjunctions used to conjoin the sentences as coordinating (coord) or correlative (corr).

   a. Both the program and the commercial were funny last night. _______________

   b. She can stop her discussion or leave. _______________

   c. I would accept either fame or money. _______________

   d. Cathy and I will travel to New York or New Jersey. _______________

3. Indicate if the conjoined elements are NPs, Advs, or Adjs.

   a. The checks are either in your wallet or on the dresser. _______________

   b. Neither tea nor lemonade quenched his thirst. _______________

   c. They played both the oboe and the sax. _______________

   d. The plant appeared healthy and green. _______________

4. Change each sentence so that it contains the appropriate correlative conjunctions. Use deletions whenever possible.

   a. He will go to Chicago, or he will stay in Memphis.

   ____

   b. Sal can't play tennis, nor can Sue.

   ____

   c. The kidnappers wanted $10,000 or the diamond ring.

   ____

   d. This child enjoys hiking and swimming.

   ____

Exercise 32

1. List three conjunctive adverbs that are used with related sentences.

   ______________ ______________ ______________

2. Write another sentence that expresses the meaning of each, using the specified construction.

   a. (Conjunctive adverb) Linda studied, but Raymond watched TV.

   ____

   b. (Coordinating conjunction) Dad was sick; nevertheless, he went to work.

   ____

   c. (Conjunctive adverb) You may have the job although you will have to work overtime.

   ____

3. Identify those of the listed complexities that are in each sentence.

Modality:	1. negation
Conjoinings:	2. conjunction
	3. disjunction
	4. alternation
	5. correlative
	6. conjunctive adv
Transformations:	7. aux or copula invers
	8. deletion

   a. The baby stumbled and fell but didn't hurt herself. ______________

   b. Bill has finished neither his homework nor his yardwork; consequently, he will stay home. ______________

   c. Both Jim and Julie are here; however, Mary hasn't arrived yet. ______________

   d. Mix the flour and the salt for the play dough. ______________

   e. Larry will do his residency in either pediatrics or family practice. ______________

   f. That actress is beautiful but not talented. ______________

   g. Dan has never lied to you, nor will he. ______________

   h. Nancy drives not only slowly, but also erratically. ______________

Exercise 30: Answers

1. conjoining, relativization, complementation, nominalization (any 3)

2. and, but, or, nor, yet (any 3)

3. a. clause: a group of words with an NP + VP (subject and predicate) that is part of a sentence
   b. independent clause: a clause which may stand alone as a complete sentence

4. the meanings must be congruous or must be related temporally

5. a. Kittie washed the clothes, and she hung them up outside.
   b. Sal bought a new car, and he drove it home.
   c. My mother gave the crystal to Ann, and she washed it.
   d. Dad fixed the chair for Mother, and she put it in the living room.

6. The identical elements have the same syntactic structure and what is deleted is clearly understood by the listener.

7. a. Adv
   b. DO
   c. Adj
   d. V
   e. S
   f. IO
   g. PN

8. a. Marvin walked south.
   Bill walked east.
   b. They displayed their pottery.
   They displayed their paintings.

9. mix, combine, between, together, same, different, alike, similar (any 3).
   These sentences are only examples. Your answers may vary.
   The bartender mixed the bourbon and water.
   Joan lives in the house between Carey and Gary.

10. a. 1
    b. 3
    c. 2

11. when one proposition is (1) in contrast to the other, (2) unexpected, or (3) contradictory (any 2)

12. a. and
    b. but
    c. but
    d. and

13. yet

14. There are two or more alternatives, or one proposition is a consequence of the other.

15. negation

16. a. verb becomes positive
    b. auxiliary inversion
    c. subject is pronominalized (any 2)

17. a. D
    b. C
    c. A
    d. A
    e. C

18. a. You may wait here, or you may wait in the secretary's office.
    b. Cecilia can't whistle, nor can she hum a tune.
    c. I must go, or I'll start to cry.
    d. Close the door and turn off the lights.
    e. Myron was articulate, but he became speechless in class.

19. a. Myra bought some, Myra bought some
    b. Felix (he), swim
    c. cleaned the yard

Exercise 31: Answers

1. either/or, neither/nor, both/and, not/but, not only/but also (any 3)

2. a. corr
   b. coord
   c. corr
   d. coord

3. a. Adv
   b. NP
   c. NP
   d. Adj

4. a. He will either go to Chicago or stay in Memphis.
   b. Neither Sal nor Sue can play tennis.
   c. The kidnappers wanted either $10,000 or the diamond ring.
   d. This child enjoys both hiking and swimming.

Exercise 32: Answers

1. however, moreover, nevertheless, therefore, consequently, subsequently (any 3)

2. a. Linda studied; however, Raymond watched TV.
   b. Dad was sick, but he went to work.
   c. You may have the job; however, you will have to work overtime.

3. a. 2, 8, 3, 8, 1
   b. 5, 1, 1, 8, 6
   c. 5, 8, 6, 1
   d. 2
   e. 5, 8
   f. 3, 1, 8
   g. 1, 4, 1, 7, 8
   h. 1, 5, 8

CHAPTER 14

Practice Test

1. List three operations used to expand sentences by combining two or more propositions in a single sentence.

______________________ ______________________ ______________________

2. List three coordinating conjunctions.

______________________ ______________________ ______________________

3. Define

   a. clause: ____

   ____

   b. independent clause: ____

   ____

4. State a condition that must exist if sentences are conjoined with *and*.

____

5. Conjoin the following pairs of sentences using personal pronouns in the second clause for the identical noun phrase(s) in the sentences.

   a. Joe saw the accident. Joe ran for the police.

   ____

   b. My aunt sold her house. A friend of mine bought the house.

   ____

   c. Dad bought a gift for the newsboy. Mom wrapped the gift.

   ____

   d. Mae picked up the papers. Mae put the papers in the trash.

   ____

6. State a condition under which identical elements may be deleted in conjoinings.

____

____

7. Identify the conjoined constituents as subjects (S), verbs (V), direct objects (DO), adjectives (Adj), adverbials (Adv), indirect objects (IO), or predicate nominatives (PN).

   a. The salmon and tuna are in the pantry. _______

   b. Dad got some candy for Grandma and Grandpa. _______

   c. They danced and laughed all night. _______

   d. Calvin drove over the mountain and through the valley. _______

   e. Tina enjoys caramels and chocolates. _______

   f. Jan became an accountant and a CPA. _______

   g. The speaker was wise and witty. _______

8. Write the sentences from which each sentence was derived.

   a. The child found his shovel and pail.

   ____

   ____

   b. Jim went to Morocco, and Carol to Tunisia.

   ____

   ____

9. List three words that may require a conjoined noun phrase in a sentence that would not be derived from two sentences. Write a sentence with a conjoined NP for each word.

   a. ________________ : ______________________________

   b. ________________ : ______________________________

   c. ________________ : ______________________________

10. Rank the sentences (using 1 for the easiest) according to their possible syntactic difficulty for children with language problems.

   a. Mom fed the dog, and she bathed it. _______

   b. The train came, and the passengers boarded. _______

   c. The girl pushed the boy, and he ran away. _______

11. State two conditions under which sentences may conjoin with *but*.

    a. ______________________________

    b. ______________________________

12. Indicate in the blank whether the sentences would be more appropriately conjoined with *and* or *but*.

    a. Sally went to the store.
       She bought a loaf of bread. _______

    b. Elliot is lazy.
       He has a job. _______

    c. Richard confessed.
       He didn't apologize. _______

    d. She listened to the boy.
       She answered his questions. _______

13. What is an alternate conjunction that could substitute for *but*?

    ____

14. State a condition necessary for sentences to be conjoined with *or*.

    ____

15. State the modality change that must be present in the first of two sentences joined with *nor*.

    ____

16. When conjoining sentences such as *Jane didn't clean the house* and *Jane didn't wash the clothes,* use *nor* and keep the auxiliary in the verb phrase. Name two changes that must be made for the second clause.

    a. ______________________________

    b. ______________________________

17. Identify the coordination as conjunction (C), disjunction (D), or alternation (A).

    a. He bought potatoes, rice, and macaroni. _______

    b. Dad could wash the glasses, but he always breaks at least one. _______

    c. Sylvia didn't go to New York, nor did she stay home. _______

    d. That model is beautiful, yet he has no sex appeal. _______

    e. That child could be sick or upset. _______

18. Conjoin the sets of sentences using the most appropriate conjunction: *but, or, nor,* or *and*. Use each conjunction listed.

    a. Pack your suitcase.
    Don't forget your toothbrush and hairdryer.

    ____

    b. Vicki was outside.
    She wasn't playing with the other children.

    ____

    c. Arthur can't dance.
    He can't play the piano. (retain *he*)

    ____

    d. You can stay.
    You can leave.

    ____

    e. The sun was shining.
    We felt raindrops.

    ____

19. Write the exact words that were deleted.

    a. The old man is out of work and has no money.

    ____

    b. Mary likes Tom's large and shaggy dog.

    ____

    c. Dad drove through Denver and into Boulder.

    ____

20. List two pairs of correlative conjunctions.

    a. ______________________________ , ______________________________

    b. ______________________________ , ______________________________

21. Identify the conjunctions used to conjoin the sentences as coordinating (coord) or correlative (corr).

    a. Janie desired neither fame nor money. ______________________________

b. Aunt Matilda and Uncle Harry will arrive on Monday or Tuesday. ____________________

c. You can sweep the floor or vacuum. ____________________

d. Both Tom and Dick are sick at home. ____________________

22. Indicate if the conjoined elements are NPs, Advs, or Adjs.

a. His glasses are either on the table or in the drawer. ____________________

b. Both Ruth and Rhoda are sick this morning. ____________________

c. Jeff was neither bored nor tired. ____________________

d. They desired neither a large house nor a fancy car. ____________________

23. Change each sentence so that it contains correlative conjunctions.

a. Joe can't have sugar, nor can Wanda.

____

b. These children enjoy sailing and canoeing.

____

c. The judge called for one stenographer or two.

____

d. We can go to the zoo or visit Uncle Phil.

____

24. List three conjunctive adverbs that are used with related sentences.

a. __________

b. __________

c. __________

25. Write another sentence that expresses the meaning of each, using the specified construction.

a. (Conjunctive adverb) My test scores are high so I should go to college.

____

b. (Coordinating conjunction) He tried to run; however, he was too terrified to move.

____

c. (Conjunctive adverb) I went to your house, but you were gone.

____

26. Identify the elaborations, conjoinings, modality changes, and transformations in each sentence by matching the numbered items to the sentence.

Modalities:
1. imperative
2. negation
3. yes-no question
4. *wh*-question

Coordination:
5. conjunction
6. disjunction
7. alternation
8. correlative
9. conjunctive adverb

Elaborations:
10. poss det or noun
11. adj modifier
12. noun adjunct

Transformations:
13. pronominal
14. reflex pro intens or reflex intens movt
15. adv preposing
16. intensifier
17. indirect obj preposing
18. *do*-support
19. contraction
20. aux or copula invers
21. prt movt
22. there
23. passive
24. deletion

a. Irene got her books out, but she didn't study. (7) ______________

b. Should the boys eat their dinner now or wait until 6:00? (5) ______________

c. Mother didn't want a diamond ring; however, she accepted it very graciously. (8) ______________

d. Either the house was struck by lightning, or someone set the fire during the storm. (3) ______________

e. When did Sue send Aunt Helen the children's gifts and luggage? (7) ______________

f. Cover your mouth, or you'll spread germs all over. (5) ______________________

g. On Monday the car was demolished and towed away, but no one was upset about it. (11) ______________________

h. Brett is going with us; therefore, Jessica can't. (5) ______________________

Chapter 14 Practice Test: Answers

1. conjoining, relativization, complementation, nominalization (any 3)

2. and, but, or, nor, yet (any 3)

3. a. clause: a group of words containing an NP + VP (subject + predicate) that is part of a sentence
   b. independent clause: a clause which may stand alone as a complete sentence

4. the meanings must be congruous or must be related temporally

5. a. Joe saw the accident, and he ran for the police.
   b. My aunt sold her house, and a friend of mine bought it.
   c. Dad bought a gift for the newsboy, and Mom wrapped it.
   d. Mae picked up the papers, and she put them in the trash.

6. The identical elements have the same syntactical structure and what is deleted is clearly understood by the listener.

7. a. S
   b. IO
   c. V
   d. Adv
   e. DO
   f. PN
   g. Adj

8. a. The child found his shovel. The child found his pail.
   b. Jim went to Morocco. Carol went to Tunisia.

9. mix, combine, between, together, same, different, alike (any 3)
   These sentences are examples only. Your answers may vary.
   Mix flour and the water.
   That boy and girl look alike.
   Mary and Dan are going together.

10. a. 3
    b. 1
    c. 2

11. when one proposition is (1) in contrast to the other, (2) unexpected, or (3) contradictory (any 2)

12. a. and
    b. but
    c. but
    d. and

13. yet

14. when there are two or more alternatives

15. negation

16. a. verb becomes positive
    b. auxiliary inversion
    c. pronominalization (any 2)

17. a. C
    b. D
    c. A
    d. D
    e. A

18. a. Pack your suitcase and don't forget your toothbrush and hairdryer.
    b. Vicki was outside, but she wasn't playing with the other children.
    c. Arthur can't dance, nor can he play the piano.
    d. You can stay, or you can leave.
    e. The sun was shining, but we felt raindrops.

19. a. The old man
    b. Mary likes Tom's dog
    c. Dad drove

20. either/or, neither/nor, both/and, not/but, not only/but also (any 2)

21. a. corr
    b. coord
    c. coord
    d. corr

22. a. Adv
    b. NP
    c. Adj
    d. NP

23. a. Neither Joe nor Wanda can have sugar.
    b. These children enjoy both sailing and canoeing.
    c. The judge called for either one stenographer or two.
    d. We can either go to the zoo or visit Uncle Phil.

24. nevertheless, however, moreover, therefore, consequently, although, subsequently (any 3)

25. a. My test scores are high; therefore, I should go to college.
    b. He tried to run, but he was too terrified to move.
    c. I went to your house; however, you were gone.

26. a. 10, 21, 6, 13, 18, 2, 19
    b. 3, 20, 10, 7, 24
    c. 18, 2, 19, 12, 9, 13, 13, 16
    d. 8, 23, 13
    e. 4, 18, 20, 17, 10, 5, 24
    f. 1, 10, 7, 13, 19
    g. 15, 23, 24, 5, 24 (the car was), 23, 24 (by someone), 6, 2, 13, 13
    h. 13, 9, 2, 19, 24 (go with us)

CHAPTER 15
Subordination

Exercise 33

1. Define dependent clause.

____

____

2. Underline the dependent clauses in the sentences and circle the subordinating conjunctions.

   a. If you brush your teeth regularly, you'll get fewer cavities.

   b. The concert was just ending as Diane drove up.

   c. Park the car wherever you can find a place.

   d. They bought the house before Eric found a job.

   e. Anna worked on her paper until dawn.

3. List three possible relationships or meanings that may be expressed in sentences joined with subordinating conjunctions.

   ____________________ ____________________ ____________________

4. Analyze the pattern of each sentence by marking off and labeling the constituents.

   a. We grew uneasy when Marty failed to come back.

   b. Greg tore the check as he removed it from the book.

   c. When she saw the lightning, Mother ran into the house.

   d. Lucy has bowled since she was a little girl.

5. Put an X after those sentences in which the adverbial clause is preposed.

   a. The plane could not land when a storm was raging. ______

   b. Dr. Winters cleaned the wound after he cut off the bandage. ______

   c. As soon as the game started, John forgot his fears. ______

d. Just after Martha had left, the letter arrived in the morning mail. ______

e. Few students borrow books from the library although it has a wide selection. ______

6. Identify the adverbial clause in the sentence as one of time, location, concession, or manner.

   a. Do not remove the cap until you're ready to use the ink. ______________________

   b. Mary wore the dress even though she didn't like it. ______________________

   c. The girls went outside after the rain had stopped. ______________________

   d. Ned speaks as though he were angry. ______________________

   e. They live where they can grow vegetables all year. ______________________

Exercise 34

1. List three words that introduce causal clauses.

   ______________ ______________ ______________

2. List two words (or co-occurring words) that introduce effect clauses.

   ______________ ______________

3. Identify the italicized phrases as the cause or effect.

   a. *Because the gas was getting low*, the doctor worried about reaching home. ______________

   b. *As the noise was excessive*, the communities near Logan Airport complained. ______________

   c. *Since he had stamina*, Arthur won the fight. ______________

   d. Lana doesn't have a car, *so she rides with Sue*. ______________

Exercise 35

1. List three words that may be used to introduce conditional clauses.

   ________________ ________________ ________________

2. Add an appropriate conditional clause to each of the following using a different conjunction in each.

   a. Open the presents now, ________________________.

   b. ________________________, you may go out with your friends.

   c. ________________________, the comma may be omitted.

3. Identify the sentence as having an adverbial clause of time, manner, location, or concession (Adv Cl); a causal clause (Caus); a conditional clause (Cond); or a clause with a conjunctive adverb (CA).

   a. Although the cake fell, the family ate it. ________________

   b. Eva is ill; she will, nevertheless, stay in school. ________________

   c. If I send that package today, it will arrive before Christmas. ________________

   d. Unless you sell 10 tickets, you won't get any for yourself. ________________

   e. She cried as if her heart were breaking. ________________

   f. He had been up two days; consequently, he drove off the road. ________________

   g. We had overslept so we were late. ________________

   h. You may leave as soon as you finish. ________________

4. Analyze the sentences by marking off and labeling the constituents.

   a. Before Lilly arrives, we'll fix up her room.

   b. The plumber came this morning because one of the pipes was leaking.

   c. After Blair receives her degree, she can become a surgical or pediatric nurse.

   d. Bob and his friends will be here before midnight if we don't have a storm.

   e. Jerry can live with us until he finishes college in June.

   f. Stella was unhappy, so she left early.

   g. You may get a book for Uncle Jack, or you may save your money.

5. Identify the listed complexities in the following sentences.

   Conjoinings: 1. disjunction
   2. conjunctive adv

   Subordination: 3. adv cl time, etc.
   4. causal clause
   5. conditional clause

   a. Bob eats all the time, yet he never gains weight because he exercises. __________

   b. Since we haven't any gas, we'll stay home this weekend. __________

   c. Although you haven't finished all your work, you will get your full allowance since you helped Mother so much. __________

   d. Whenever it rains, it pours; nevertheless, you must go on if you want to succeed. __________

   e. Since we have lived in this area, the price of houses has tripled; consequently, we expect to make money when we sell our house. __________

   f. Leo will quit as soon as he earns $500, but he really needs more for clothes if he goes to college this fall. __________

   g. After a two-week vacation, you should feel rested, provided you don't do too much. __________

Exercise 33: Answers

1. Dependent clause: a group of words introduced by a subordinating conjunction and consisting of an NP + VP that cannot stand alone as a sentence.

2. a. if you brush your teeth regularly
   b. as Diane drove up
   c. wherever you can find a place
   d. before Eric found a job
   e. no adv clause

3. condition, concession, location, cause/effect or causality, manner, time, purpose (any 3)

4. a. (NP) We / (V_L) grew / (Adj) uneasy / (Adv) when Marty failed to come back.
   b. (NP^1) Greg / (V) tore / (NP^2) the check / (Adv) as he removed it from the book.
   c. (Adv) When she saw the lightning / (NP) Mother / (V_i) ran / (Adv) into the house.
   d. (NP) Lucy / (V_i) has bowled / (Adv) since she was a little girl.

5. c, d

6. a. time
   b. concession
   c. time
   d. manner
   e. location

Exercise 34: Answers

1. because, since, as, for (any 3)

2. so, so that

3. a. cause
   b. cause
   c. cause
   d. effect

Exercise 35: Answers

1. if, provided that, unless, so long as (any 3)

2. These answers are examples only. Your answers may vary.
   a. *If* you want to.
   b. *Provided* you finish your work
   c. *Unless* it's setting off the date

3. a. Adv Cl
   b. CA
   c. Cond
   d. Cond
   e. Adv Cl
   f. CA
   g. Caus
   h. Adv Cl

4. a. Adv / NP^1 / V / NP^2
   Before Lilly arrives / we / 'll fix up / her room.
   b. NP / V_i / Adv / Adv
   The plumber / came / this morning / because one of the pipes was leaking.
   c. Adv / NP^1 / V_L / NP^1
   After Blair receives her degree / she / can become / a surgical or pediatric nurse.
   d. NP / V_{be} / Adv / Adv / Adv
   Bob and his friends / will be / here / before midnight / if we don't have a storm.
   e. NP / V_i / Adv / Adv
   Jerry / can live / with us / until he finishes college in June.
   f. NP / V_L / Adj / NP / V_i / Adv
   Stella / was / unhappy / (so) / she / left / early.
   g. NP^1 / V / NP^2 / Adv / NP / V / NP^2
   You / may get / a book / for Uncle Jack / (or) / you / may save / your money.

5. a. 1, 4
   b. 4
   c. 3, 4
   d. 3, 2, 5
   e. 3, 2, 3
   f. 3, 1, 5
   g. 5

CHAPTER 15

Practice Test

1. Define dependent clause.

____

____

2. Underline the dependent clause in each sentence and circle the subordinating conjunction.

   a. David and Lynn will marry before she finishes college.

   b. We found the car where he had left it.

   c. The supervisor looked as if he meant business.

   d. When the sirens sound, everyone leaves the streets.

3. List three possible relationships or meanings that are in sentences joined with subordinating conjunctions.

   a. ____________________

   b. ____________________

   c. ____________________

4. Analyze the pattern of each sentence by marking off and labeling the constituents.

   a. They didn't change the plans because everyone seemed content.

   b. Call me as soon as you arrive.

   c. Barry went into town since he had time to spare.

   d. A high wind arose, so the bay was not safe.

   e. Although Jack has been sick, he is giving a party for his mother when she retires.

   f. Mary and Joan have been friends since they were in college.

5. Put an X after those sentences in which the adverbial clause is preposed.

   a. When you visit Newport, you must see Ocean Drive. __________

   b. Our car runs well since we had the engine overhauled. __________

c. The river had risen considerably during the night. __________

d. If you exercise regularly, you'll stay in good condition. __________

e. After the accident, Eddie acted as though he didn't remember anything. __________

6. Identify the adverbial clause in the sentence as one of time, location, concession, or manner.

a. The men work hard although they are paid little. __________

b. Before you pay the bill, check the gas meter. __________

c. Wherever Cynthia went, the dog followed. __________

d. Kurt is drinking as though he were dehydrated. __________

e. The team members played as if they were tired. __________

7. List three words that introduce causal clauses.

__________ __________ __________

8. List two words (or co-ocurring words) that introduce effect clauses.

__________ __________

9. Put an X after those sentences that have shiftable clauses.

a. People were starving as a result of the famine. __________

b. Our boys won because they played harder. __________

c. Meat prices skyrocketed after the drought. __________

d. Carla didn't like it here so she went back to Oregon. __________

e. Put away your toys before you go to bed. __________

10. Identify the italicized phrases as the cause or effect.

a. Burt worked all night *because he wanted the job completed on time*. __________

b. The storm left a coating of sleet on the highway, *so we decided to postpone our shopping spree*. __________

c. The ice on the pond thawed *since the sun was hot*. __________

d. *As the groceries were delivered late*, we didn't eat until 7:00. __________

11. List three words that may be used to introduce conditional clauses.

________________ ________________ ________________

12. Add an appropriate conditional clause to each of the following using a different conjunction in each.

    a. ________________________________, don't worry about it.

    b. You can go to the movie ________________________________.

    c. ________________________________, you will surely win the award.

13. Identify each sentence as having an adverbial clause of time, concession, manner, or location (Adv Cl); a conditional clause (Cond); a causal clause (Caus), or a conjunctive adverb (CA).

    a. Mother arrived on time although the train was late. ________________

    b. If you are careful, you won't make any errors. ________________

    c. After George rang the doorbell, the boys yelled, "Trick or Treat!" ________________

    d. I can't give you the car keys since you have been grounded. ________________

    e. You may go shopping; moreover, you may get a dress. ________________

    f. I will lend Bill the money provided he pays me back. ________________

    g. There was a lot of excitement while she was at lunch. ________________

    h. Jake was saddened by the news; nevertheless, he pretended not to care. ________________

14. Identify all the modality changes, conjoinings, elaborations, and transformations in the sentences.

Modalities:	1. imperative
	2. negation
	3. yes-no question
	4. *wh*-question
Coordination:	5. conjunction
	6. disjunction
	7. alternation
	8. correlative
	9. conjunctive adverb
Subordination:	10. adv cl of time, etc.
	11. causal clause
	12. conditional clause
Elaborations:	13. poss det or noun
	14. adj modifier
	15. noun adjunct

Transformations: 16. pronominal
17. reflex pro intens or reflex intens movt
18. adv preposing
19. intensifier
20. indirect obj preposing
21. *do*-support
22. contraction
23. aux or copula invers
24. prt movt
25. there
26. passive
27. deletion

a. Although Jack doesn't like chicken, he cleaned his plate and asked for seconds. (9)

____

b. Why wasn't the dog walked after it was fed? (10)

____

c. Can the girls go to the movies if Mother gives them their allowance? (6)

____

d. Because Reggie turned the term paper in so late, he received a *C*, but he passed the course and graduated. (10)

____

e. When you see Zora in New York, give her a big hug and tell her hello. (11)

____

f. As Dad fertilized last week, the grass has grown and there are new buds on the roses. (5)

____

g. Heimo is either very tired, or possibly he is very upset about something. (6)

____

Chapter 15 Practice Test: Answers

1. Dependent clause: a group of words introduced by a subordinating conjunction and consisting of an NP + VP that cannot stand alone as a sentence

2. a. <u>before</u> she finishes college
   b. <u>where</u> he had left it
   c. <u>as if</u> he meant business
   d. <u>when</u> the sirens sound

3. time, manner, location, concession, purpose, condition, cause/effect (any 3)

4. NP^1 V NP^2 Adv
   a. They / didn't change / the plans / because everyone seemed content.
   NP^1 V NP^2 Adv
   b. (   ) / Call / me / as soon as you arrive.
   NP V_i Adv Adv
   c. Barry / went / into town / since he had time to spare.
   NP V_i NP V_L Adj
   d. A high wind / arose / (so) / the bay / was / not safe.
   Adv NP^1 V NP^2 Adv Adv
   e. Although Jack has been sick / he / is giving / a party / for his mother / when she retires.
   NP^1 V_L NP^1 Adv
   f. Mary and Joan / have been / friends / since they were in college.

5. a, d

6. a. concession
   b. time
   c. location
   d. manner
   e. manner

7. because, since, as, for (any 3)

8. so, so that

9. b, e

10. a. cause
    b. effect
    c. cause
    d. cause

11. if, so long as, provided, unless (any 3)

12. These answers are examples only. Your answers may vary.
    a. *If* you don't finish
    b. *provided* you finish your homework
    c. *Unless* you lose the last race

13. a. Adv Cl
    b. Cond
    c. Adv Cl
    d. Caus
    e. CA
    f. Cond
    g. Adv Cl
    h. CA

14. a. 10, 18, 21, 2, 22, 16, 13, 5, 27
    b. 4, 23, 2, 22, 26, 27, 10, 16, 26, 27
    c. 3, 23, 12, 20, 16, 13
    d. 11, 18, 15, 24, 19, 16, 6, 16, 5, 27
    e. 10, 18, 16, 1, 20, 16, 14, 5, 1, 20, 16
    f. 11, 18, 5, 25, 14
    g. 8, 19, 18, 16, 19, 16

CHAPTER 16

Relativization

Exercise 36

1. List three relative pronouns and two relative adverbs.

   a. ______________________ d. ______________________

   b. ______________________ e. ______________________

   c. ______________________

2. Explain the function of a relative clause in a sentence.

   ____

   ____

3. Underline the relative clause in each sentence and draw an arrow from the relative clause introducer to the noun referent.

   a. We saw the elephant that was born at the zoo.

   b. The blunders that the speaker made indicated her nervousness.

   c. The boy who enlisted is my cousin.

   d. We noticed a barn that looked deserted.

   e. Do you have the tools that you need for changing tires?

4. Write the matrix sentence on the first line and the insert sentence on the second.

   a. Put the box in the closet where the dog can't get it.

      M: ____

      I: ____

   b. Children who are not yet five may enter free.

      M: ____

      I: ____

c. That's the girl whose name I misspelled.

M: ______________________________

I: ______________________________

d. He is one employee whom everyone trusts.

M: ______________________________

I: ______________________________

e. Helen's aunt is a nurse who works at St. Vincent's Hospital.

M: ______________________________

I: ______________________________

f. This is the hat that belongs to Mr. Andrews.

M: ______________________________

I: ______________________________

5. Write one sentence, embedding the second sentence into the first. Use a different relative pronoun in each. (Use a relative adverb whenever possible.)

a. M: That boy is sleepy in school.
   I: That boy works nights.

____

b. M: Bob is going to school at Georgetown University.
   I: There is a good law school at Georgetown University.

____

c. M: He located the article.
   I: He needed the article for his paper.

____

d. M: The carton broke open.
   I: The carton contained the crayons.

____

6. Underline the relative clause and identify [1] its syntactic environment as final (F) or medial (M); [2] whether the pronoun is a subject or subject modifier replacement (S), direct object replacement (DO), indirect object replacement (IO), or an NP in an adverbial replacement (Adv); and [3] whether it is prep-fronted (P-F).

   a. Ms. Bridgeman is the woman to whom he should give the report. ________ ________ ________

   b. The money that Don lost has been repaid. ________ ________ ________

   c. Mother found the shawl that had belonged to Grandma. ________ ________ ________

   d. Evelyn, whose apartment was ransacked, has moved to a new neighborhood. ________ ________ ________

   e. The town in which they work is Kingston. ________ ________ ________

7. Write a sentence for each that would reflect the wrong meaning received by a reader using an S-V-O surface order strategy.

   a. The animal that bit the child was rabid.

   ____

   b. The tower of blocks which had been built on the table toppled over.

   ____

   c. Jack's mother, who received a refund from the store owner, was satisfied.

   ____

Exercise 37

1. Write the complete relative clause before reduction putting parentheses around the deleted words.

   a. The books the boy returned were torn.

   ____

   b. The car Janice bought was in good condition.

   ____

   c. The youth educated at Stanford became a lawyer.

   ____

   d. Those dogs running around the streets will be picked up.

   ____

2. Underline the postnominal modifier resulting from a relative clause reduction in each sentence and identify it as a *V-ing* phrase, *V-en* phrase, appositive (appos), or prep phrase (PP).

   a. The boy on the bench is the captain. ____________________

   b. Joseph, a member for five years, was elected treasurer. ____________________

   c. The officer caught the children playing hooky from school. ____________________

   d. The tumbleweeds tossed about by the wind piled up near the fence. ____________________

   e. Joan has a cat without a tail. ____________________

3. Explain the different meanings that the writer could be conveying in the following sentences. Identify each as having a restrictive (R) or nonrestrictive (NR) clause.

   a. The second-year students who are industrious will graduate this spring.

   ____

   ____

   b. The second-year students, who are industrious, will graduate this spring.

   ____

   ____

4. Write two sentences, one with a restrictive relative clause and one with a nonrestrictive relative clause.

   Restrictive: ____________________________________

   Nonrestrictive: __________________________________

5. Underline the prenominal modifier(s) in each sentence and identify it as an Adj, *-en* participle, *-ing* participle, or noun adjunct (NA).

   a. Fragrant roses grew in her flower garden. ____________________

   b. A shifted participle is a prenominal modifier. ____________________

   c. The chirping birds woke up the sleeping children. ____________________

   d. That scented stationery is a birthday gift. ____________________

   e. The ripped-out pages angered the old librarian. ____________________

6. Write the relative clause before reductions for each of the pre- or postnominal modifiers.

   a. Soiled linen was strewn around the floor.

   ____

   b. He swatted at the fly annoying him.

   ____

   c. The adjusted price goes into effect today.

   ____

7. Analyze the sentences by marking off and labeling the constituents.

   a. The scissors in the top drawer of that cabinet are kitchen shears.

   b. That boy running down the street must have pushed the little girl that is crying.

   c. Whenever he sees a mouse, that brave-looking little cat runs into any closet he can find.

   d. My brother from New York is never happy when he is away from home.

   e. The coat you are looking for is in the closet in the hall near the front door.

8. Identify the operations used to generate the sentences using only those listed.

   1. rel pro
   2. rel pro + movt
   3. rel pro del
   4. rel adv + movt
   5. rel pro + *be* deletion
   6. prep + rel pro movt
   7. participle movt
   8. adj movt

   a. The girl practicing on the balance beam is not a gymnast. ______________

   b. Susan, to whom Jack gave a ring, is out of the country now. ______________

   c. The driver in the red car looks mysterious. ______________

   d. We tasted the cheesecake that Mario made. ______________

   e. The glistening water was tempting for the young children. ______________

   f. That damaged package arrived the other day when you were out. ______________

   g. The party at the club last week honored Jason Jackson, a famous poet. ______________

9. Write noun phrases for each list of words, putting the adjectives (or modifiers) and determiners in the correct order.

   a. favorite, one of, TV, that is on Sunday, my, shows

   ____

   b. heavy, her, thermal, in the top drawer, underwear

   ____

   c. charming, most, the, ladies, young, two of, who are on the team

   ____

10. Identify only the listed elaborations and transformations in the sentences.

Elaborations:	1. poss det or noun
	2. adj modifier
	3. noun adjunct
	4. relative clause
	5. *-ing* or -en part modifier
	6. prep phr modifier
	7. appositive
Transformations:	8. pronominalization
	9. passive
	10. deletion

   a. The shifting winds brought in the rain that we needed.

   ____

   b. The boy with the black eye walked into class holding his hand over his eye.

   ____

   c. The car, a battered old wreck, is in a garage in Mapleton.

   ____

   d. The child beaten in the fight at school is in the intensive care unit.

   ____

   e. People from Portland often ski in those high mountains you can see from here.

   ____

Exercise 36: Answers

1. Relative Pronouns: who, whose, which, whom, that (any 3)
   Relative Adverbs: where, when

2. Relative clauses expand NPs and function to restrict or limit the meaning or to provide additional information about the NP.

3. a. elephant ← that was born at the zoo
   b. blunders ← that the speaker made
   c. boy ← who enlisted
   d. barn ← that looked deserted
   e. tools ← that you need for changing tires

4. a. M: Put the box in the closet.
      I: The dog can't get the box in the closet.
   b. M: Children may enter free.
      I: Children are not yet five.
   c. M: That is the girl.
      I: I misspelled the girl's name.
   d. M: He is one employee.
      I: Everyone trusts one employee.
   e. M: Helen's aunt is a nurse.
      I: The nurse (Helen's aunt) works at St. Vincent's Hospital.
   f. M: This is the hat.
      I: The hat belongs to Mr. Andrews.

5. a. That boy who works nights is sleepy in school.
   b. Bob is going to school at Georgetown University where there is a good law school.
   c. He located the article which he needed for his paper.
   d. The carton that contained the crayons broke open.

6. a. (to) whom he should give the report — F, IO, P-F
   b. that Don lost — M, DO
   c. that had belonged to Grandma — F, S
   d. whose apartment was ransacked — M, S
   e. in which they work — M, Adv, P-F

7. a. The child was rabid.
   b. The table toppled over.
   c. The store owner was satisfied.

Exercise 37: Answers

1. a. (that/which) the boy returned
   b. (that/which) Janice bought
   c. (that was/who was) educated at Stanford
   d. (that/which are) running around the streets

2. a. on the bench, PP
   b. a member for five years, appos
   c. playing hooky from school, V-ing phrase
   d. tossed about by the wind, V-en phrase
   e. without a tail, PP

3. a. *only* the second-year students who are industrious will graduate this spring, R
   b. all the second-year students are industrious, and they graduate in the spring, NR

4. These answers are examples only. Your answers may vary.
   a. restrictive: Babies who are born prematurely must be put in incubators.
   b. nonrestrictive: Mr. Brown, who is an architect, designed our house.

5. a. fragrant: Adj, flower: NA
   b. shifted: -en part, prenomial: Adj
   c. chirping: -ing part, sleeping: -ing part
   d. scented: -en part, birthday: NA
   e. ripped out: -en part, old: Adj

6. a. which/that was soiled
   b. which/that was annoying him
   c. which/that was adjusted

NP^1 V_L NP^1
7. a. The scissors in the top drawer of that cabinet / are / kitchen shears.
NP^1 V NP^2
b. That boy running down the street / must have pushed / the little girl that is crying.
Adv NP V_i Adv
c. Whenever he sees a mouse / that brave-looking little cat / runs / into any closet that he can find.
NP V_L Adv Adj Adv
d. My brother from New York / is / never / happy / when he is away from home.
NP V_{be} Adv
e. The coat you are looking for / is / in the closet in the hall near the front door.

8. a. 5
b. 6
c. 5, 5, 8
d. 2
e. 5, 7, 5, 8
f. 5, 7, 4
g. 5, 5, 5, 8

9. a. one of my favorite TV shows that is on Sunday
b. her heavy thermal underwear in the top drawer
c. two of the most charming young ladies who are on the team

10. a. 5, 4, 8, 8
b. 6, 2, 5, 1, 1
c. 7, 5, 2, 9, 10, 6
d. 5, 9, 10, 6, 2, 3
e. 6, 2, 4, 10, 8

CHAPTER 16

Practice Test

1. List three relative pronouns and two relative adverbs.

   a. ______________________

   b. ______________________

   c. ______________________

   d. ______________________

   e. ______________________

2. Explain the function of a relative clause in a sentence.

   ____

   ____

3. Underline the relative clause modifier in each sentence and draw an arrow from the relative pronoun to the noun to which the clause is related (or modifies).

   a. That's the boy who dated Monica.

   b. The drugstore that's on Maple Avenue carries that brand.

   c. There is the car that I want to buy.

   d. Esther is the girl whom you met at my house.

   e. Is this the recording that Jim wants?

   f. The town in which we were living was tiny.

4. Write the matrix sentence on the first line and the insert sentence on the second.

   a. The man who is mayor of our town is seeking re-election.

      M: ____

      I: ____

   b. Those students who intend to work in science must study mathematics.

      M: ____

      I: ____

c. The class will be in the morning when the children are all here.

M: ____________________

I: ____________________

d. The dog that barks at the mail carrier is really quite friendly.

M: ____________________

I: ____________________

e. Angela saw a movie that made her cry.

M: ____________________

I: ____________________

f. The store in which we were shopping today is going out of business.

M: ____________________

I: ____________________

5. Write a sentence, embedding the second sentence into the first. (Use a relative adverb when possible.)

a. M: The boys climbed the pole.
   I: The pole had been greased.

____

b. M: Mother bought the chair.
   I: She saw the chair at the mall last week.

____

c. M: The man was a crook.
   I: Dad gave a check to the man.

____

d. M: Ms. Gibbs shops in Hecht's.
   I: She can always find her size in Hecht's.

____

6. Underline the relative clause and identify [1] its syntactic environment as final (F) or medial (M); [2] whether the pronoun is a subject or subject modifier replacement (S), direct object replacement (DO), indirect object replacement (IO), or NP in an adverbial replacement (Adv); and [3] whether it is prep-fronted (P-F).

a. The goal for which we are striving is world peace. ________ ________ ________

b. A marathon which drew runners from around the world was held in Ohio. __________ __________ __________

c. Janet finally got the job that she wanted. __________ __________ __________

d. Dr. Smith is a man whom everyone admires. __________ __________ __________

e. The woman to whom Harry gave the corsage is allergic to flowers. __________ __________ __________

7. Write a sentence(s) for each that would reflect the wrong meaning received by a reader using a surface order strategy.

a. The woman who spoke to Mr. Johnson is a judge.

____

b. The glass which he left on the table was broken.

____

c. The boy who was hit by that man died.

____

8. Write the complete relative clause and put parentheses around the deleted words.

a. These are the boys I was looking for.

____

b. The alternative you suggested is no longer viable.

____

c. The bus coming up the road is going to the fairgrounds.

____

9. Underline the words resulting from a relative clause reduction in each sentence and identify each as a *V-ing* phrase, *V-en* phrase, prep phrase, or appositive.

a. The fine imposed upon the man was $500.

____

b. The police officer arrested the boys throwing stones at the windows.

____

c. The clock in the kitchen was a gift.

____

d. The boy smoking a cigarette will be put off the team.

____

e. Helen, my sister, is beautiful.

____

10. Explain two different meanings that the writer could be conveying in the following sentences. Identify the clause as restrictive (R) or nonrestrictive (NR).

    a. Flies, which carry the nagana parasite, are dangerous to humans.

    ____

    b. Flies which carry the nagana parasite are dangerous to humans.

    ____

11. Write two sentences, one with a restrictive clause and one with a nonrestrictive relative clause.

    a. Restrictive: ______________________________

    b. Nonrestrictive: ______________________________

12. Underline the prenominal modifier(s) in each sentence and identify each as an Adj, *-ing* part, or *-en* part.

    a. The dripping water annoyed father.

    ____

    b. The wounded soldier lay in the field.

    ____

    c. The perspiring children dashed into the cool water.

    ____

    d. The rioting mob trampled the blockades.

    ____

    e. No one can fix these shattered glasses.

    ____

13. Identify the operations used to generate the sentences, using only those listed.

    1. rel pro
    2. rel pro + movt
    3. rel pro del
    4. rel adv + movt
    5. rel pro + *be* deletion
    6. prep + rel pro movt
    7. participle shift
    8. adj shift

    a. Karen feels sorry for the woman sitting by herself.

    ____

    b. Todd, a gregarious fellow, makes friends with everyone he meets.

    ____

    c. Nancy bought the Subaru last month when her other car gave out.

    ____

    d. Leaking oil on pavements dampened by rain may cause problems.

    ____

    e. The car in the driveway belongs to my uncle who is here from Massachusetts.

    ____

    f. The field on which the game was played looked very green.

    ____

    g. The boxes which we packed had been broken open when they were in transit.

    ____

    h. The place where Barbara has her office is 30 miles from her home in Springfield.

    ____

    i. Set those books you brought for me on that table near the door and come on in.

    ____

14. Write the relative clause before reductions for each pre- or postnominal modifier.

    a. The hills covered with snow were lovely in the moonlight.

    ____

b. A weeping woman stood outside the door.

____

c. The coins in the bracelet are extremely old.

____

15. Analyze the sentences by marking off and labeling the constituents.

    a. The giggling girls in the first class annoyed the other children this morning when they were having a test.

    b. The doctor we go to has been a specialist in internal medicine for a long time.

    c. The bracelet you gave me must be on that shelf in the bathroom where I took my shower.

    d. The man standing on the ledge leaped at noon when everyone was walking to lunch.

    e. The attractive usher in the blue dress seemed upset when that man walked over to her.

16. Write a noun phrase for each list of words, putting the adjectives (or modifiers) and determiners in the correct order.

    a. grey, skirt, my, that I bought in Paris, long, chiffon

    ____

    b. two, coins, small, those, gold, in the drawer

    ____

    c. blue, bowl, that, lovely, which Uncle Roy gave us, Swedish

    ____

17. Identify all the modality changes, conjoinings, elaborations, and transformations in each sentence.

Modalities:	1. imperative
	2. negation
	3. yes-no question
	4. *wh*-question
Coordination:	5. conjunction
	6. disjunction
	7. alternation
	8. correlative
	9. conjunctive adv
Subordination:	10. adv cl of time, etc.
	11. causal cl
	12. conditional cl

Elaborations:
13. poss det or noun
14. adj modifier
15. noun adjunct
16. relative clause
17. *-ing* or *-en* participle modifier
18. prep phrase modifier
19. appositive

Transformations:
20. pronomial
21. reflex pro intens or reflex intens movt
22. adv preposing
23. intensifier
24. indirect obj preposing
25. *do*-support
26. contraction
27. aux or copula invers
28. prt movt
29. there
30. passive
31. deletion

a. Did you like the present Dad bought for you? (7)

____

b. The car that was damaged by that drunk driver was towed to a garage near John's home. (8)

____

c. Eliza saw the dog playing in the street, and she locked it up in the garage. (5)

____

d. After the boys have a big dinner, why do they always do things that are so strenuous? (11)

____

e. If Penny buys the chest she saw at the antique shop, my father can fix the broken drawer. (10)

____

f. Barking dogs and screaming children annoy that old man who is sitting on the steps. (7)

____

g. Val hasn't sent Brad those gifts that were wrapped a week ago. (7)

____

h. Their sister, a shy blushing bride, was rejected by her husband, and became not only agressive, but hard. (11)

____

Chapter 16 Practice Test: Answers

1. Pronouns: who, whose, which, whom, that (any 3)
   Adverbs: when, where

2. Relative clauses expand noun phrases and function to restrict or limit the meaning of the NP they follow or provide additional information about the NP.

3. a. boy ← who dated Monica
   b. drugstore ← that's on Maple Avenue
   c. car ← that I want to buy
   d. girl ← whom you met at my house
   e. recording ← that Jim wants
   f. town ← in which we were living

4. a. M: The man is seeking re-election.
      I: The man is mayor of our town.
   b. M: Those students must study mathematics.
      I: Those students intend to work in science.
   c. M: The class will be in the morning.
      I: The children are all here in the morning.
   d. M: The dog is really quite friendly.
      I: The dog barks at the mail carrier.
   e. M: Angela saw a movie.
      I: The movie made her cry.
   f. M: The store is going out of business.
      I: We were shopping in the store today.

5. a. The boys climbed the pole which had been greased.
   b. Mother bought the chair that she saw at the mall last week.
   c. The man to whom Dad gave a check was a crook.
   d. Ms. Gibbs shops in Hecht's where she can always find her size.

6. a. for which we are striving — M, Adv, P-F
   b. which drew runners from around the world — M, S
   c. that she wanted — F, DO
   d. whom everyone admires — F, DO
   e. to whom Harry gave the corsage — M, IO, P-F

7. a. Mr. Johnson is a judge.
   b. The table was broken.
   c. The boy hit that man. That man died.

8. a. (that/whom) I was looking for
   b. (that/which) you suggested
   c. (that is/which is) coming up the road

9. a. imposed on the man: *V-en* phr
   b. throwing stones at the windows: *V-ing* phr
   c. in the kitchen: prep phr
   d. smoking a cigarette: *V-ing* phr
   e. my sister: appositive

10. a. *all* flies carry the parasite, *and* are dangerous to humans (nonrestrictive)
    b. *only* flies carrying the parasite are dangerous to humans (restrictive)

11. These answers are only examples. Your answers may vary.
    a. restrictive: Girls who are age 6 or above may join.
    b. nonrestrictive: My father, who lived in New York City for years, likes the country.

12. a. dripping: *-ing* part
    b. wounded: *-en* part
    c. perspiring: *-ing* part, cool: Adj
    d. rioting: *-ing* part
    e. shattered: *-en* part

13. a. 5
    b. 5, 5, 8, 2, 3
    c. 4
    d. 5, 7, 5, 5
    e. 5, 1
    f. 6
    g. 2
    h. 4, 5
    i. 2, 3, 5

14. a. which were covered with snow
    b. who was weeping
    c. that are in the bracelet

NP^1 V NP^2 Adv

15. a. The giggling girls in the first class / annoyed / the other children / this morning when they were having a test.

    NP^1 V_L NP^1 Adv

    b. The doctor we go to / has been / a specialist in internal medicine / for a long time.

    NP V_{be} Adv

    c. The bracelet you gave me / must be / on that shelf in the bathroom where I took my shower.

    NP V_i Adv

    d. The man standing on the ledge / leaped / at noon when everyone was walking to lunch.

    NP V_L Adj Adv

    e. The attractive usher in the blue dress / seemed / upset / when that man walked over to her.

16. a. my long grey chiffon skirt that I bought in Paris
    b. those two small gold coins in the drawer
    c. that lovely blue Swedish bowl which Uncle Roy gave us

17. a. 3, 25, 27, 20, 16, 31, 20
    b. 16, 20, 30, 14, 30, 31, 18, 13
    c. 17, 5, 20, 20, 28
    d. 10, 22, 14, 4, 25, 27, 20, 22, 16, 20 (rel pro), 23
    e. 12, 22, 16, 31, 20, 15, 13, 17, 30, 31
    f. 17, 5, 31, 17, 14, 20, 16
    g. 2, 26, 24, 20, 16, 30, 31
    h. 13, 19, 14, 17, 30, 13, 5, 31, 8, 2, 31

CHAPTER 17

Comparatives

Exercise 38

1. Underline the comparative and superlative forms of the adjectives and adverbs and specify the degree as comparative (C) or superlative (S).

   a. My schoolwork is much harder than it was last year. ____________

   b. Lloyd speaks more intelligibly than Willa. ____________

   c. Please be a little quieter. ____________

   d. The baby had a worse cold than Sherry did. ____________

   e. Of the three universities, Harvard has the largest endowment. ____________

   f. Gayle is the most efficient secretary in the pool. ____________

   g. This tool is really more versatile than the other. ____________

   h. That movie was not the best one on TV last night. ____________

   i. Which container holds less gas? ____________

2. Indicate with ∧ where the optionally deleted word would go and write the word in the blank.

   a. Bill exercised more strenuously than Jerry. ____________

   b. A television as old as that one shouldn't work. ____________

   c. Electricians make as much money as doctors. ____________

   d. We want dogs larger than our neighbors'. ____________

   e. Movies as dull as those shouldn't be shown. ____________

3. Underline the expanded adverbial or adjective and identify it as an adverbial (Adv) or an adjective (Adj).

   a. This class is not as interesting as the other. ____________

   b. The white paint gets used up more quickly than the blue. ____________

   c. The sunrise could not have been more beautiful than it was this morning. ____________

d. More swiftly than a fleeting deer, Bob sped across the field. ______________________

e. I've never seen hair more lovely than Mary's. ______________________

f. This material looks more durable than that you're holding. ______________________

g. A car as defective as Mary's is not safe to drive around the corner. ______________________

h. Jean works the least efficiently in the late afternoons. ______________________

4. Underline the complete noun phrases containing comparative constructions.

   a. I tell as few secrets as possible to Amy.

   b. You should keep jewelry as valuable as that in the safest place in the house.

   c. Fewer boys than anticipated came, so we had more girls than we needed.

   d. As frequently as possible, Mother goes to the best beauty salon in town.

   e. Dick eats twice as many calories as any of us, but he is the least overweight member of the team.

   f. We will work for as many days as we can.

   g. The more active of the children have been involved in the fewest accidents.

5. Analyze the sentences by marking off and labeling the constituents.

   a. A boy with a nose as large as Billy has should be a good sleuth.

   b. Our cat looks as fierce as a lion when she's stalking a mouse.

   c. As boldly as a brave warrior, David walked to the stage.

   d. A man that has as much incentive as Mr. Allen should hold a job more successfully than he does.

   e. As talented a singer as Abby could have been in the contest that we had last week.

   f. The most beautiful cars in the lot may not be the most practical.

6. Identify only the listed complexities in each sentence.

Elaborations:
1. adjective modifier
2. comparative
3. relative clause
4. prep phr modifier

Transformation:
5. deletion

a. If you work as hard as you can, you could win the highest prize in the contest.

____

b. As smart a boy as Ken should get higher grades than he does.

____

c. The girl who was the lightest player on the team played more roughly than the others.

____

d. The engine runs more smoothly than before, but it sounds about as bad as it did.

____

e. Jean has more friends than Jill, but she changes friends more often than Jill does.

____

Exercise 38: Answers

1. a. harder, C
   b. more intelligibly, C
   c. quieter, C
   d. worse, C
   e. largest, S
   f. most efficient, S
   g. more versatile, C
   h. best, S
   i. less, C

2. a. than Jerry ∧ (exercised or did)
   b. than one ∧ (is)
   c. doctors ∧ (make or do)
   d. neighbors' ∧ (dogs or are)
   e. dull as those ∧ (are)

3. a. as interesting as the other, Adj
   b. more quickly than the blue, Adv
   c. more beautiful than it was this morning, Adj
   d. more swiftly than a fleeting deer, Adv
   e. more lovely than Mary's, Adj
   f. more durable than that you're holding, Adj
   g. as defective as Mary's, Adj
   h. the least efficiently, Adv

4. a. as few secrets as possible
   b. jewelry as valuable as that, the safest place in the house
   c. Fewer boys than anticipated, more girls than we needed
   d. the best beauty salon in town
   e. twice as many calories as any of us, the least overweight member of the team
   f. as many days as we can
   g. the more active of the children, the fewest accidents

5. a. (NP^1 / V_L / NP^1) A boy with a nose as large as Billy has / should be / a good sleuth.
   b. (NP / V_L / Adj / Adv) Our cat / looks / as fierce as a lion / when she's stalking a mouse.
   c. (Adv / NP / V_i / Adv) As boldly as a brave warrior / David / walked / to the stage.
   d. (NP^1 / V / NP^2 / Adv) A man that has as much incentive as Mr. Allen / should hold / a job / more successfully than he does.
   e. (NP / V_{be} / Adv) As talented a singer as Abby / could have been / in the contest that we had last week.
   f. (NP^1 / V_L / NP^1) The most beautiful cars in the lot / may not be / the most practical.

6. a. 2, 5, 1, 2, 4
   b. 2, 1, 5, 1, 2, 5
   c. 3, 1, 2, 2, 5
   d. 2, 5, 2, 5
   e. 2, 5, 2, 5

CHAPTER 17

Practice Test

1. Underline the comparative and superlative forms of the adjectives and adverbs and specify the degree as comparative (C) or superlative (S).

   a. This is the fanciest restaurant in town. ______________________

   b. Which of the three hats would be the most appropriate? ______________________

   c. John expects to have a better time this year. ______________________

   d. This engine performs least adequately. ______________________

   e. The dog growled more threateningly when Tom put out his hand. ______________________

   f. Bristol is the southernmost city in Virginia. ______________________

   g. This week Crystal arrived on time more often. ______________________

   h. Our math teacher asks the trickiest questions. ______________________

   i. We were more pleasantly greeted by Tim's family. ______________________

2. Indicate with ^ where the optional deletion is and write it in the blank.

   a. A man as busy as Dr. White has no time for his family. ______________________

   b. These girls attend church more regularly than I. ______________________

   c. They will buy a smaller house than that one when they retire. ______________________

   d. A boy who studied as much as Craig should have graduated with honors. ______________________

   e. Nancy spends half as much money for food as Betty. ______________________

3. Underline the expanded adverbial or adjective and identify it as an adverbial (Adv) or adjective (Adj).

   a. Jack is high scorer more often than Jerry. ______________________

b. The girls completed their projects less successfully than the boys did. ______________________

c. Hands as dirty as yours are a disgrace. ______________________

d. Mary's score was higher on the balance beam than in the floor exercise. ______________________

e. I haven't read any poems more brilliant than Mary's. ______________________

f. Bill performed the most satisfactorily. ______________________

g. More often than not, Dad gets home after 6:00. ______________________

h. A dog as devoted as his is would be a pleasure. ______________________

4. Underline the complete noun phrases containing comparative constructions.

a. The hardest tests sometimes require the least amount of study.

b. In the most difficult situations, Luci is the more helpful of the two children.

c. As alert a dog as that should be a very good watchdog.

d. Kavi carries the heaviest load, but he gets more As than anyone else.

e. Children as mischievous as they are possibly need a more challenging program.

f. The worst time of the year is the middle of winter.

g. He can't buy the same kind of car as he has now for less money than he paid before.

5. Analyze the sentences by marking off and labeling the constituents.

a. The temperature hasn't been as high as it is now in the last 15 years.

b. If Tom got more right answers than Sally, he must have solved some problems inaccurately because he got a lower grade.

c. A dog that barks as much as Rollo should have gone to obedience school for a longer time.

d. A tennis player as good as Beth is must be the most valuable person you have on the team.

e. The girls who are the best singers in our class have not been in the choir for as long as some of the poorer singers.

6. Identify all the modality changes, conjoinings, elaborations, and transformations in the sentences.

Modalities:	1. imperative	
	2. negation	
	3. yes-no question	
	4. *wh*-question	
Coordination:	5. conjunction	
	6. disjunction	
	7. alternation	
	8. correlative	
	9. conjunctive adv	
Subordination:	10. adv cl of time, etc.	
	11. causal cl	
	12. conditional cl	
Elaborations:	13. poss det or noun	17. *-ing* or *-en* participle modifier
	14. adj modifier	18. prep phrase modifier
	15. noun adjunct	19. appositive
	16. relative cl	20. comparative
Transformations:	21. pronominal	27. contraction
	22. reflex pro intens or reflex intens movt	28. aux or copula invers
	23. adv preposing	29. prt movt
	24. intensifier	30. there
	25. indirect obj preposing	31. passive
	26. *do*-support	32. deletion

a. Don't buy a rug as large as that for a room that is so small. (11)

____

b. If you were more industrious, you could read that book you didn't finish. (11)

____

c. How much faster than a boar can a female deer run? (5)

____

d. I can read this biography more easily than that novel since the print is larger. (5)

____

e. Not much money is saved today when people are making more money than they ever did because prices have gone up accordingly. (10)

____

f. Will Tim buy Mary the largest diamond he can find, or will he get a ring that has a smaller stone? (16)

____

g. Working mothers in our company don't take as much time off as other women and often they themselves are managing a home. (13)

____

Chapter 17 Practice Test: Answers

1. a. fanciest, S
   b. most appropriate, S
   c. better, C
   d. least adequately, S
   e. more threateningly, C
   f. southernmost, S
   g. more often, C
   h. trickiest, S
   i. more pleasantly, C

2. a. Dr. White ∧ (is)
   b. than I ∧ (do or attend)
   c. than that one ∧ (is)
   d. as Craig ∧ (did or studied)
   e. as Betty ∧ (does or spends)

3. a. more often than Jerry, Adv
   b. less successfully than the boys did, Adv
   c. as dirty as yours, Adj
   d. higher on the balance beam than in the floor exercise, Adj
   e. more brilliant than Mary's, Adj
   f. the most satisfactorily, Adv
   g. more often than not, Adv
   h. as devoted as his is, Adj

4. a. The hardest tests, the least amount of study
   b. the most difficult situations, the more helpful of the two children
   c. As alert a dog as that
   d. the heaviest load, more As than anyone else
   e. Children as mischievous as they are, a more challenging program
   f. The worst time of the year
   g. the same kind of car as he has now, less money than he paid before

5. a. The temperature (NP) / hasn't been (V_L) / as high as it is now (Adj) / in the last 15 years (Adv).
   b. If Tom got more right answers than Sally, (Adv) / he (NP^1) / must have solved (V) / some problems (NP^2) / inaccurately (Adv) / because he got a lower grade (Adv).
   c. A dog that barks as much as Rollo (NP) / should have gone (V_i) / to obedience school (Adv) / for a longer time (Adv).
   d. A tennis player as good as Beth is (NP^1) / must be (V_L) / the most valuable person that you have on the team (NP^1).
   e. The girls who are the best singers in our class (NP) / have not been (V_{be}) / in the choir (Adv) / for as long as some of the poorer singers (Adv).

6. a. 1, 26, 2, 27, 20, 14, 21, 32, 16, 21, 24
   b. 23, 12, 21, 20, 21, 16, 32, 21, 26, 2, 27
   c. 4, 20, 32, 28, 15
   d. 21, 20, 32, 11, 20
   e. 2, 31, 32, 16, 20, 21, 23, 26, 32, 11
   f. 3, 28, 25, 14, 20, 16, 32, 21, 7, 3, 28, 21, 16, 21, 14, 20
   g. 17, 18, 13, 26, 2, 27, 20, 29, 32, 5, 23, 21, 22

CHAPTER 18

Language Analysis III Exercise

Complete both syntactic and semantic descriptions and summaries of the following hypothetical sample. Use the analysis in chapter 18 as a guide.

Language Sample

1. Before Grandpa was operated on, did he always sit in the house and complain, or could he walk with his cane then?
2. The boy Jenny slapped is the smartest boy in our class, but nobody likes him.
3. The place where Timmy lives must be real big because he has two horses that he can ride.
4. This blue parka is warmer than that green parka, so why can't I take it to the mountains?
5. Those two boys running down the street threw stones into Mr. Allen's fountain, and he was very mad.

Syntactic Description

1. Before Grandpa was operated on, did he always sit in the house and complain, or could he walk with his cane then?

   VP modulation:

   NP modulation:

   Conjoining:

   Elaboration:

   Transformation:

2. The boy Jenny slapped is the smartest boy in our class, but nobody likes him.

   VP modulation:

NP modulation:

Modality:

Conjoining:

Elaboration:

Transformation:

3. The place where Timmy lives must be real big because he has two horses that he can ride.

VP modulation:

NP modulation:

Conjoining:

Elaboration:

Transformation:

4. This blue parka is warmer than that green parka, so why can't I take it to the mountains?

VP modulation:

NP modulation:

Modality:

Conjoining:

Elaboration:

Transformation:

5. Those two boys running down the street threw stones into Mr. Allen's fountain, and he was very mad.

   VP modulation:

   NP modulation:

   Conjoining:

   Elaboration:

   Transformation:

Syntactic Summary

Sentence Frames	*Frequency of Occurrence*	*Comments*
Pattern 1 (intransitive verb)	__________	__________
Pattern 2 (transitive verb)	__________	__________
Pattern 3 (linking verb)	__________	__________
Pattern 4 (linking verb)	__________	__________
Verb Phrase Modulations		
irregular past	__________	__________
regular past	__________	__________
irregular 3rd pers sing	__________	__________

Verb Phrase Modulations	*Frequency of Occurrence*	*Comments*
regular 3rd pers sing	__________	__________
uncontracted copula	__________	__________
modal	__________	__________
be auxiliary	__________	__________
preposition	__________	__________
particle	__________	__________
Noun Phrase Modulations		
+ def article	__________	__________
Ø article	__________	__________
cardinal	__________	__________
demonstrative	__________	__________
regular plural	__________	__________
Modality Changes		
yes-no question	__________	__________
wh-question	__________	__________
negation	__________	__________
Conjoining		
conjunction	__________	__________
disjunction	__________	__________
alternation	__________	__________
causal clause	__________	__________
adv clause	__________	__________
Elaboration		
poss determiner	__________	__________
poss noun	__________	__________
adjective	__________	__________
relative clause	__________	__________
-ing participle modifier	__________	__________
comparative	__________	__________
Transformation		
aux inversion	__________	__________
do-support	__________	__________
pronominalization:		
personal	__________	__________
indefinite	__________	__________
relative	__________	__________
contraction	__________	__________
deletion	__________	__________
adverbial preposing	__________	__________
passive	__________	__________
intensifier	__________	__________

Semantic Description

1. Before Grandpa was operated on, did he always sit in the house and complain, or could he walk with his cane then?

2. The boy Jenny slapped is the smartest boy in our class, but nobody likes him.

3. The place where Timmy lives must be real big because he has two horses that he can ride.

4. This blue parka is warmer than that green parka, so why can't I take it to the mountains?

5. Those two boys running down the street threw stones into Mr. Allen's fountain, and he was very mad.

Semantic Summary

Number of utterances:

Number of propositions:

Number of propositions per utterance:

Noun cases	*Frequency of Occurrence*
Agent	__________
Mover	__________
Experiencer	__________
Patient	__________
Entity	__________
Equivalent	__________
Possessor	__________
Verb cases	
Action	__________
Process	__________
Stative	__________

Modifier cases	*Frequency of Occurrence*
Size	______
Condition	______
Cardinal	______
Color	______
Quality	______
Adverbial cases	
Location	______
Time	______
Reason	______
Frequency	______
Instrument	______
Intensifier	______

Language Analysis III Exercise: Answers

Syntactic Description

1. Before Grandpa was operated on, did he always sit in the house and complain, or could he walk with his cane then?

   $NP + V_i + Adv + Adv$,
   $NP + V_i + Adv + Adv$

   VP modulation: *be* aux
   particle
   preposition (2)
   modal
   NP modulation: Ø art
   +def art
   Modality: yes-no question (2)
   Conjoining: conjunction
   adv cl (time)
   alternation
   Elaboration: poss det
   Transformation: adv preposing (2)
   passive
   do-support
   del (with passive) + (conjunction) (2)
   pers pronom (2)
   aux invers (2)

2. The boy Jenny slapped is the smartest boy in our class, but nobody likes him.

   $NP^1 + V_L + NP^1 + Adv$,
   $NP^1 + V + NP^2$

   VP modulation: reg past
   uncontr copula
   reg 3rd sing
   preposition
   NP modulation: +def art (2)
   Ø art
   Modality: negation
   Conjoining: disjunction (*but*)
   Elaboration: rel clause
   adjective
   poss det
   comparative
   Transformation: del (rel pro)
   indef pronom
   pers pronom

3. The place where Timmy lives must be real big because he has two horses that he can ride.

   $NP + V_L + Adj + Adv$

VP modulation:	reg 3rd sing
	modal (2)
	irreg 3rd sing
NP modulation:	+def art
	Ø art
	card
	reg plural
Conjoining:	causal cl
Elaboration:	rel adv cl
	rel cl
Transformation:	intens (*real*)
	pers pronom (2)
	relative pro

4. This blue parka is warmer than that green parka, so why can't I take it to the mountains?

   $NP + V_L + Adj$,
   $NP^1 + V + NP^2 + Adv + Adv$

VP modulation:	uncontr copula
	modal
	preposition
NP modulation:	dem (2)
	+def art
	reg plural
Modality:	negation
	wh-question
Conjoining:	causal cl (*so*)
Elaboration:	adj modifier (2)
	comparative
Transformation:	del (is warm)
	aux invers
	contraction
	pers pronom (2)

5. Those two boys running down the street threw stones into Mr. Allen's fountain, and he was very mad.

   $NP^1 + V + NP^2 + Adv$,
   $NP + V_L + Adj$

VP modulation:	irreg past
	uncontr copula
	prep (2)
NP modulation:	dem
	card
	+def art
	Ø art (2)
	reg pl (2)
Conjoining:	conjunction
Elaboration:	*-ing* participle phr modifier
	poss noun
Transformation:	intens
	pers pronom

Syntactic Summary

Sentence Patterns	*Frequency of Occurrence*	*Comments*
Pattern 1 (intrans verb)	2	
Pattern 2 (trans verb)	3	
Pattern 3 (linking verb)	3	
Pattern 4 (linking verb)	1	
Verb Phrase Modulations		
irregular past	1	
regular past	1	
irregular 3rd pers sing	1	has
regular 3rd pers sing	2	
uncontracted copula	3	is, was
modal	4	could, can, must
be aux	1	was (passive)
preposition	6	in, with, to, into, down
particle	1	on, with trans verb
Noun Phrase Modulations		
+ def article	6	the
Ø article	5	
cardinal	2	two
demonstrative	3	this, that, those
regular plural	4	
Modalities		
wh-question	1	in conjoined sentence
yes-no question	2	in alternation
negation	2	in contraction, *no*body
Conjoinings		
conjunction	2	conjoined verbs conjoined sentences
disjunction	1	but
alternation	1	or
causal	2	because, so
adverbial clause	1	time (before)
Elaborations		
poss determiner	2	his, our
poss noun	1	
adjective	3	
relative clause	3	that deletion (2) where deletion (1)
-ing participle modifier	1	postnominal, participle, + prep phr
comparative	2	reg superlative, reg comparative + than

Transformations	*Frequency of Occurrence*	*Comments*
auxiliary inversion	3	in yes-no, in *wh*-question
do-support	1	in question
pronominalization:		
personal	8	he, him, I, it
indefinite	1	nobody
relative	1	that (also rel adv *where*)
contraction	1	modal
deletion	4	in passive, in comp, rel pro, conjoined verbs
adverbial preposing	2	adv clause
passive	1	agent deletion in adv cl
intensifier	2	real, very

Semantic Description

1. Before Grandpa was operated on, did he always sit in the house and complain, or could he walk with his cane then?

Grandpa sit house always sometime	Entity—stative—location—frequency—time
Grandpa complain always sometime	Mover—action—frequency—time
someone operate on Grandpa	Agent—action—patient
Grandpa have cane	Possessor—process—patient
Grandpa walk (with) cane then	Mover—action—instrument—time

2. The boy Jenny slapped is the smartest boy in our class, but nobody likes him.

boy be boy class	Entity—stative—equivalent—location
Jenny slap boy	Agent—action—patient
boy be smart	Entity—stative—quality
someone have class	Possessor—process—patient
somebody like boy	Experiencer—process—patient

3. The place where Timmy lives must be real big because he has two horses that he can ride.

place be real big (for some reason)	Entity—stative—intensifier—size—reason
Timmy live place	Entity—stative—location
Timmy have (two) horse	Possessor—process—(card)—patient
Timmy ride horse	Agent—action—patient

4. This blue parka is warmer than that green parka, so why can't I take it to the mountains?

parka be warm	Entity—stative—quality
parka be blue	Entity—stative—color
parka be warm	Entity—stative—quality
parka be green	Entity—stative—color
someone take parka (to) mountain for some reason	Agent—action—patient—location—reason

5. Those two boys running down the street threw stones into Mr. Allen's fountain, and he was very mad.

(two) boy throw stone fountain	Agent—action—patient—location
Mr. Allen have fountain	Possessor—process—patient
boy run street	Mover—action—location
Mr. Allen be (very) mad	Entity—stative—intensifier—condition

Semantic Summary

	Frequency of Occurrence
Noun cases	
Agent	5
Mover	3
Experiencer	1
Patient	10
Entity	10
Equivalent	1
Possessor	4
Verb cases	
Action	8
Process	5
Stative	10
Modifier cases	
Size	1
Condition	1
Cardinal	1
Color	2
Quality	3
Adverbial cases	
Location	6
Time	3
Reason	2
Frequency	2
Instrument	1
Intensifier	2

CHAPTERS 1–18

Review Test

1. Analyze the sentences by marking off and labeling the constituents.

   a. The dog John ran over must have been the stray that's been in the neighborhood all week.

   b. When he was young, my father came to the U.S. because he wanted a good job.

   c. Mother is going to a place where she can sit in the sun all day.

   d. Jason will be in school during the summer, but Mary will work since she needs money for clothes.

   e. Before the children settled down, they had destroyed all the toys Jack had gotten for them.

   f. Both that left end and the quarterback have been in more games than the rest of the team.

   g. The youngest child in the class seems smarter than the other children.

   h. Someone must have stolen the books you put in my locker last week.

   i. All the money that I have saved is in a bank located in my old hometown.

   j. Birds as rare as that could become extinct unless we protect them.

   k. A book as important as that should be a bestseller.

2. Identify each italicized word by using the numbered list.

1. determiner	6. adverb
2. pronoun	7. particle
3. preposition	8. auxiliary
4. adjective	9. verb
5. intensifier	10. conjunction

   a. He *always* arrives *before* five in the morning. ____________________

   b. I know *nothing* about *that*. ____________________

   c. She knitted that *lovely* sweater for *herself*. ____________________

   d. They *may* get here when John is leaving. ____________________

   e. My paper is better *than* yours is. ____________________

   f. I saw *her* this morning *when* she left for work. ____________________

g. The woman was *quite* annoyed *about* her bill. ____________________

h. The weather will improve *after* February *or* March. ____________________

i. He brought *her* dog with him. ____________________

j. I haven't *seen* Dad *since* 6:00 a.m. ____________________

k. The work *that* he did was *extremely* difficult. ____________________

l. The plane on *which* she left was a 707. ____________________

m. The players *who* were on the bench *are* in the showers. ____________________

n. They *are* working *hard* now. ____________________

o. Jane's throat felt *worse* at dinnertime. ____________________

p. She is *so* weak *every* evening. ____________________

q. It was late so I left, but I can try *out* your car later. ____________________

r. We *have* been outside *since* Dad left for work. ____________________

s. Pick me *up* in the morning. ____________________

t. Sean *did* all the tasks *which* the course required. ____________________

u. Jim cleaned up the house *after* the guests left. ____________________

3. Circle and label the noun phrases that are subjects (S), direct objects (DO), indirect objects (IO), or predicate nominatives (PN) of the main verb in each sentence.

a. Both Alice and Jean are coming to our party next week. ____________________

b. A boy in my class should have been the one they picked for the lead. ____________________

c. That dog you found makes more noise than I can endure. ____________________

d. Children as young as they are should take longer naps than thirty minutes. ____________________

e. A girl I didn't like in high school became my closest friend after we graduated. ____________________

f. When the task is interesting, boys as mischievous as they are often complete their work with no fooling around. ____________________

g. The guests who left this morning gave both Mother and me some beautiful towels for our bathrooms. ____________________

h. The next meeting we have will be the last one at which we can consider the proposal. ____________________

i. A man that was a complete stranger carried three bags of groceries to the car for me. ____________________

4. Identify all the modality changes, conjoinings, elaborations, and transformations in the sentences by matching the appropriate numbers to the sentences.

Modalities:	1. imperative
	2. negation
	3. yes-no question
	4. *wh*-question
Coordination:	5. conjunction
	6. disjunction
	7. alternation
	8. correlative
	9. conjunctive adv
Subordination:	10. adv cl time, etc.
	11. causal cl
	12. conditional cl
Elaborations:	13. poss det or noun
	14. adj modifier
	15. noun adjunct
	16. relative clause
	17. *-ing* or *-en* participle modifier
	18. prep phrase modifier
	19. appositive
	20. comparative
Transformations:	21. pronominal
	22. reflex pro intens or reflex intens movt
	23. adv preposing
	24. intensifier
	25. indirect obj preposing
	26. *do*-support
	27. contraction
	28. aux or copula invers
	29. prt movt
	30. there
	31. passive
	32. deletion

a. Who was that man working in your yard while you were away? (5) ____________________

b. Tom hurt himself this morning when he dived into the pool, and he was taken to a hospital in Atlanta. (8) ____________________

c. Because Lola didn't finish her dress she's staying home from the party Don is having. (10) ______________________

d. Can the cars damaged in the wreck be repaired, or must they be scrapped? (13) ______________________

e. Tim is not as smart as Bill, but he is more talented. (6) ______________________

f. Either Sam or Nancy must make Grandma some chicken soup if Mother isn't home by noon. (7) ______________________

g. Fix that leaking faucet in the bathroom, or Dad will be quite upset, and you won't be given your allowance. (13) ______________________

h. Is there anything you must get before you leave on your trip around the world? (11) ______________________

i. The most interesting book Daphne read was rather long, but she finished it in two days. (8) ______________________

5. Read the paragraphs and fill in the blanks.

Farmer Jones, the richest farmer in the valley, was upset! A wolf that had come into the yard at night had killed 30 of his best chickens. So Farmer Jones offered a pouch filled with wine to anyone who could kill the wolf.

a. A noun phrase that is an indirect object ______________________

b. An appositive in the paragraph ______________________

c. The first postnominal modifier that is a complete relative clause

____

d. A postnominal modifier that is a participle phrase

____

e. The second noun phrase that contains a superlative adjective

____

f. The second noun phrase with a full relative clause

____

g. The semantic relationship expressed in the main proposition in the first sentence

____

h. The proposition and semantic relationships of the first embedding in the second sentence

____

The next morning, Bill, Tom, and Jack got up very early. They drove to Mr. Frank's home and sat where they were hidden by an elm tree. Tom stayed in the car, which they had parked down the street. Mr. Frank drove out of his garage, and Tom started the car as quietly as he could. He followed Mr. Frank until they approached the dock.

i. An adverbial clause of location

____

j. The semantic relationships expressed in the first part of the fourth sentence

____

k. The verb phrase that contains a nontruncated passive

____

l. One of the independent clauses in a sentence with conjunction

____

m. An adverbial phrase containing a comparative expansion

____

n. A preposed adverbial

____

o. A relative clause in the paragraph

____

p. An adverbial clause denoting duration

____

6. Complete syntactic and semantic descriptions of the following language sample. In the semantic description, state the underlying propositions in each sentence and the semantic relationships.

   a. Dad caught the mouse that ran across Mom's foot.

   Syntactic Description *Semantic Description*

b. You should wash your car because it's dirty.

Syntactic Description *Semantic Description*

c. When I'm bigger, Dad will give me those boots, and then I can climb up the mountain.

Syntactic Description *Semantic Description*

d. Giraffes are animals with long necks, so they can eat the leaves on the trees.

Syntactic Description *Semantic Description*

Chapters 1-18 Review Test: Answers

NP^1 V_L NP^1
1. a. The dog John ran over / must have been / the stray that's been in the neighborhood all week.

Adv NP V_i Adv Adv
b. When he was young, / my father / came / to the U.S. / because he wanted a good job.

NP V_i Adv
c. Mother / is going / to a place where she can sit in the sun all day.

NP V_{be} Adv Adv NP V_i Adv
d. Jason / will be / in school / during the summer, / (but) Mary / will work / since she needs money for clothes.

Adv NP^1 V NP^2
e. Before the children settled down, / they / had destroyed / all the toys Jack had gotten for them.

NP V_{be} Adv
f. Both that left end and the quarterback / have been / in more games than the rest of the team.

NP V_L Adj
g. The youngest child in the class / seems / smarter than the other children.

NP^1 V NP^2
h. Someone / must have stolen / the books you put in my locker last week.

NP V_{be} Adv
i. All of the money I have saved / is / in a bank located in my old hometown.

NP V_L Adj Adv
j. Birds as rare as that / could become / extinct / unless we protect them.

NP^1 V_L NP^1
k. A book as important as that / should be / a bestseller.

2. a. 6, 3
   b. 2, 2
   c. 4, 2
   d. 8
   e. 10
   f. 2, 6
   g. 5, 3
   h. 3, 10
   i. 1
   j. 9, 3
   k. 2, 5
   l. 2
   m. 2, 9
   n. 8, 6
   o. 4
   p. 5, 1
   q. 10, 7
   r. 8, 10
   s. 7
   t. 9, 2
   u. 10

3. a. Both Alice and Jean: S
   b. A boy in my class: S,
      the one they picked for the lead: PN
   c. That dog you found: S,
      more noise than I can endure: DO
   d. Children as young as they are: S,
      longer naps than thirty minutes: DO
   e. A girl I didn't like in high school: S,
      my closest friend: PN
   f. boys as mischievous as they are: S,
      their work: DO
   g. The guests who left this morning: S,
      both Mother and me: IO,
      some beautiful towels for our bathrooms: DO
   h. The next meeting we have: S,
      the last one at which we consider the proposal: PN
   i. A man that was a complete stranger: S,
      three bags of groceries: DO

4. a. 4, 17, 13, 10, 21
   b. 21, 16, 21, 5, 21, 31, 32, 18
   c. 11, 23, 26, 2, 27, 13, 21, 27, 16, 32
   d. 3, 28, 31, 32, 17, 31, 32, 7, 3, 28, 21, 31, 32
   e. 20, 2, 32, 6, 21, 20
   f. 8, 32, 25, 15, 12, 2, 27
   g. 1, 17, 18, 7, 24, 5, 21, 25, 2, 27, 31, 32, 13
   h. 3, 28, 30, 21, 16, 32, 21, 10, 21, 13, 18
   i. 14, 20, 16, 32, 24, 6, 21, 21

5. a. anyone who could kill the wolf
   b. the richest farmer in the valley
   c. that had come into the yard at night
   d. filled with wine
   e. 30 of his best chickens
   f. anyone who could kill the wolf
   g. Entity—stative—condition
   h. A wolf had come into the yard at night,
      Mover—action—location—time
   i. where they were hidden by an elm tree
   j. Mover—action—location,
      Possessor—process—patient
   k. were hidden by an elm tree
   l. Mr. Frank drove out of his garage (or)
      Tom started the car as quietly as he could
   m. as quietly as he could
   n. The next morning
   o. which they had parked down the street
   p. until they approached the dock

6. a. Dad caught the mouse that ran across Mom's foot.
   $NP^1 + V + NP^2$

   Syntactic

VP modulation:	irreg past (2), prep
NP modulation:	Ø art (2), +def art
Elaboration:	rel clause, poss noun
Transformation:	rel pro

   Semantic

Dad caught the mouse:	Agent—action—patient
mouse ran across foot:	Mover—action—location
Mom has a foot:	Entity—stative—part

   b. You should wash your car because it's dirty.
   $NP^1 + V + NP^2 + Adv$

   Syntactic

VP modulation:	modal, contr copula
Conjoining:	causal cl (subordination)
Elaboration:	poss det
Transformation:	pers pronom (2), contraction

   Semantic

   (someone) wash car (for some reason):
   Agent—action—patient—reason
   (someone) have car:
   Possessor—process—patient
   car be dirty:
   Entity—stative—condition

c. When I'm bigger, Dad will give me those boots, and then I can climb up the mountain.
$NP^1 + V + NP^2 + Adv + Adv$,
$NP + V_i + Adv + Adv$
Syntactic

VP modulation:	contr copula, modal (2), prep
NP modulation:	Ø art, dem, +def art, reg plural
Conjoining:	(subordination) adv cl time, (coordination) conjunction
Elaboration:	comparative
Transformation:	pers pronom (3), adv preposing (2) ind obj preposing, contraction

Semantic
Dad give boot someone *sometime:*
Agent—action—patient—beneficiary—time
someone be big(er):
Entity—stative—size
someone climb mountain then:
Mover—action—location—time

d. Giraffes are animals with long necks so they can eat the leaves on the trees.
$NP^1 + V_L + NP^1 + Adv$ or $NP^1 + V_L + NP^1$ and $NP^1 + V + NP^2$
Syntactic

VP modulations:	uncontr copula, modal, prep (2)
NP modulations:	Ø art (3), +def art (2), reg plural (4), irreg pl (1)
Conjoining:	coordination (*so* cl)
Elaboration:	prep phr modifier (2), adjective
Transformation:	pers pronom

Semantic

giraffe be animal:	Entity—stative—equivalent
girafffe eat leaf:	Agent—action—patient
the necks are long:	Entity—stative—size
animal have neck for some reason:	Entity—stative—part—reason
leaves are on trees:	Entity—stative—location

CHAPTER 19

Nominalization and Complementation

Exercise 39

1. Identify the voice or voice and aspect of the infinitive phrases.

	Voice	*Aspect*
a. to be dreaming	__________	__________
b. to have been completed	__________	__________
c. to be bathed	__________	__________
d. to ring	__________	__________
e. to have been practicing	__________	__________
f. to have turned on	__________	__________

2. Analyze the constituents of the infinitive phrases by marking off and labeling them.

   a. to take off ten pounds

   b. to feel brave

   c. to have been in school today

   d. to eat at noon

   e. to remain friends

   f. to be cautious

   g. to have been turning

3. State the feature necessary in verbs so that they may have infinitives as complements.

   ____

4. Identify the object of the verb in each sentence as an infinitive phrase (IP), noun phrase + infinitive phrase (NP + IP), or accusative pronoun + inf phrase (AP + IP).

   a. The Chens must prefer to go to the mountains. ________________

b. Mother is always urging Dad to play golf. ____________________

c. Jeff must have wanted them to stay at home. ____________________

d. The baby started to cry about midnight. ____________________

e. The teacher should allow her to leave early. ____________________

5. Indicate with an X those verbs that may be followed immediately by infinitive complements as direct objects.

a. travel __________

b. begin __________

c. like __________

d. let __________

e. attempt __________

f. feel __________

g. advise __________

h. intend __________

i. prefer __________

j. enjoy __________

k. tell __________

l. direct __________

m. fail __________

n. hesitate __________

6. Write the propositions in the deep structure for each sentence and the semantic relationships for each proposition.

a. The supervisor expected the crew to work hard.

____

____

b. The class planned to build a fort behind the school.

____

____

c. Dad wanted me to be a doctor.

____

____

7. Put an X after those verbs that require an NP different from the subject of the main verb as the subject of the infinitive.

a. continue	______	f. tempt	______	k. postpone	______
b. allow	______	g. challenge	______	l. teach	______
c. help	______	h. deserve	______	m. learn	______
d. remember	______	i. advise	______		
e. direct	______	j. lead	______		

8. Write the infinitive phrase in each sentence and include the infinitive marker for each.

   a. Dad heard us come in last night.

   ____

   b. Mother intends to make a salad for the picnic next week.

   ____

   c. The colonel wants to retire to a place where the sun shines every day.

   ____

   d. The woman felt a cold chill spread over her body.

   ____

   e. The coach intended for the team to spend an extra day in New York.

   ____

   f. The leader made the scouts fend for themselves.

   ____

Exercise 40

1. Write the propositions and the semantic relationships of the propositions expressed in each sentence.

   a. The stew was too salty for the family to eat.

   ______________________ : ______________________

   ______________________ : ______________________

b. The girls bought a basket in which to put the fruit.

_______________ : _______________

_______________ : _______________

c. To become a doctor Dick studied for years.

_______________ : _______________

_______________ : _______________

2. Circle those adjectives that can have infinitive complements without an intensifier to qualify the adjective.

a. ready
b. glad
c. smart
d. eager
e. hasty
f. sorry
g. cold
h. woody
i. impossible
j hot
k. fat

3. Underline the infinitive phrase in each sentence and identify its function as direct object (NP^2), predicate nominative (NP^1), subject (NP^1), or adverbial of purpose (Adv).

a. To finish his homework, Tim stayed home last night. _______________

b. Mary's intent was to send invitations to all her co-workers. _______________

c. The mail carrier wanted to deliver all his mail before noon. _______________

d. To hear about his trip to Russia should be very interesting. _______________

e. The children must have started to make the popcorn for the party. _______________

4. Write each complete infinitive phrase contained in the sentences adding *to* in those phrases in which it is omitted.

a. Dad advised Pepe to go get a new battery.

____

b. The excitement made her forget to complain about her problems.

____

c. Did June remember to watch Riley put on the tire?

____

5. Identify the main verb, the subject of the main verb, the infinitive verb, and the subject of the infinitive.

   a. I considered the movie silly.
   b. The men were too lazy to finish the work.
   c. Penny wants a dog for the children to play with.
   d. The manager asked Jim to work overtime.
   e. To win a gold medal is every athlete's dream.
   f. The team lost the opportunity to play in the tournament.
   g. The scout should help the old woman cross the street.

	Main Verb	*Subject*	*Infinitive*	*Subject*
a.	____	____	____	____
b.	____	____	____	____
c.	____	____	____	____
d.	____	____	____	____
e.	____	____	____	____
f.	____	____	____	____
g.	____	____	____	____

6. Match the infinitive (phrase) in each sentence to the appropriate syntactic functions.

   1. Inf compl: obj of verb
   2. NP + inf compl
   3. Accus pro + inf compl
   4. for. . .to inf compl
   5. deletion
   6. Adj + inf compl
   7. Intens + Adj + inf compl
   8. Inf compl: predicate nominative
   9. Inf phrase as subject
   10. Inf compl of quasi-modal
   11. Inf of purpose
   12. Inf compl of *NP*
   13. Passive inf

   a. David wanted me to caddy for him. ____________
   b. Jack is watching the team practice. ____________
   c. To climb a mountain is a great experience. ____________
   d. Our class is going to be given a party. ____________
   e. Mary is flying to New York to meet her guests from Sweden. ____________
   f. The weather is too humid to eat outside. ____________
   g. Bob's ability to sleep anywhere upsets the teacher. ____________

h. Mother's wish was for the wedding to be held in the garden. ______________________

i. Harry likes for Ruth to dress in the latest style. ______________________

j. Her idea was to vacation at the beach. ______________________

k. Dad made my older brother go to a state college. ______________________

l. Lucy is eager to become a nurse. ______________________

Exercise 41

1. Analyze the constituents in the participle phrases by marking off and labeling them.

   a. staying healthy after 60

   b. riding your bike along the trail

   c. exercising at home every day

   d. being in the dark all the time

   e. remaining friends in spite of constant arguments

   f. eating three meals every day

2. Write (P) in the blank if the verb can be immediately followed by a participle only, (PI) if the verb can be followed by a participle or infinitive complement, and (I) if the verb can only have infinitive complements; leave blank if the verb can have none of the above.

a. detest ____________	e. recommend ____________	i. match ____________
b. neglect ____________	f. practice ____________	j. escape ____________
c. mind ____________	g. see ____________	k. prefer ____________
d. agree ____________	h. dare ____________	

3. Write the subject of the participle nominalization in the blank.

   a. Mary is a good student, but her bragging about her grades annoys everyone. ______________________

   b. The coach was upset about the team's losing their first game in the tournament. ______________________

   c. It will soon be time for Dad and Harry to go hunting. ______________________

d. Both of the girls dislike doing housework. ______________________

e. Carrying in all the groceries herself tired Nancy. ______________________

f. The teacher gave the children directions about caring for the gerbils. ______________________

g. The police arrested two boys for breaking into the school. ______________________

4. Underline the complete participle nominalization in each sentence and identify its function as subject (S), direct object (DO), predicate nominative (PN), or object of a preposition (OP).

   a. My brother earns extra money by mowing our neighbors' lawns. ______________________

   b. Buying food for our family takes most of my paycheck. ______________________

   c. Jeri's hobby is collecting shells from different beaches. ______________________

   d. His interning at County Hospital was a good experience. ______________________

   e. Nora considered investing some money in gold coins. ______________________

   f. The problem was finding someone to take care of the children. ______________________

   g. Mother hates Dad's working overtime. ______________________

   h. For cleaning out the garage, Mr. Rinaldo gave Tom five dollars. ______________________

5. Identify the underlying propositions in the sentence and the semantic relationships for each. Give the major proposition first.

   a. Andrea loves hiking in the mountains.

   ______________________ : ______________________

   ______________________ : ______________________

   b. John exercises every day by running around the mall.

   ______________________ : ______________________

   ______________________ : ______________________

6. Identify only the listed complexities in the sentences.

Noun Phrase Elaborations:
1. relative clause
2. participle phrase modifier
3. infinitive nominalization/complementation
4. participle nominalization/complementation

Transformations:
5. indirect object preposing
6. passive
7. deletion

a. The girls considered going to the sale that was being held by the alumni. ____________

b. The teacher scolded the children fighting in the sandbox. ____________

c. My mother made me go get some more ice cream. ____________

d. The students the principal selected for the committee are being excused early. ____________

e. The children's bickering is bothering the babysitter. ____________

f. My dad decided to quit playing poker for such high stakes. ____________

g. To get all As is becoming an obsession with Tom. ____________

h. Emma loves going to Washington to ski in the Cascades. ____________

i. Ms. Block's dressing to impress other people is costing a fortune. ____________

j. Gary is going to wash his hair before starting to study. ____________

k. Dad is going to be here to see Tom play in the tournament next week. ____________

l. By driving 55 mph you should be able to get to Richmond in a couple of hours. ____________

m. The teacher asked Ron to help Jimmy check the math problems. ____________

n. Mother's dream was for Tim to be accepted to medical school. ____________

o. Don was happy to hear about John's leaving school without graduating. ____________

p. The girl crying about losing her lunch money was playing in the street. ____________

Exercise 39: Answers

1. a. active, progressive
   b. passive, perfect
   c. passive
   d. active
   e. active, perfect progressive
   f. active, perfect

2. a.
   V NP^2
   to take off / ten pounds
   b.
   V_L Adj
   to feel / brave
   c.
   V_{be} Adv Adv
   to have been / in school / today
   d.
   V_i Adv
   to eat / at noon
   e.
   V_L NP^1
   to remain / friends
   f.
   V_L Adj
   to be / cautious
   g.
   V_i
   to have been turning

3. Catenation

4. a. IP
   b. NP + IP
   c. AP + IP
   d. IP
   e. AP + IP

5. b, c, e, h, i, m, n

6. a. supervisor expect (something):
      Experiencer—process—complement
      crew work hard: Mover—action—manner
   b. class plan (something):
      Experiencer—process—complement,
      class build fort school:
      Agent—action—complement—location
   c. Dad want (something):
      Experiencer—process—complement,
      someone be doctor: Entity—stative—equivalent

7. b, c, e, f, g, i, j, l

8. a. (to) come in last night
   b. to make a salad for the picnic next week
   c. to retire to a place where the sun shines every day
   d. (to) spread over her body
   e. to spend an extra day in New York
   f. (to) fend for themselves

Exercise 40: Answers

1. a. the stew was too salty:
      Entity—stative—intensifier—condition,
      the family eat the stew: Agent—action—patient
   b. the girls bought a basket: Agent—action—patient,
      the girls (will) put the fruit in the basket:
      Agent—action—patient—locative
   c. Dick studied for years for some reason:
      Experiencer—process—duration—reason
      Dick became a doctor: Entity—stative—equivalent

2. a, b, c, d, e, f

3. a. to finish his homework, Adv
   b. to send invitations to all her co-workers, NP^1
   c. to deliver all his mail before noon, NP^2
   d. to hear about his trip to Russia, NP^1
   e. to make the popcorn for the party, NP^2

4. a. to go get a new battery,
      (to) get a new battery
   b. (to) forget to complain about her problems,
      to complain about her problems
   c. to watch Riley put on the tire,
      (to) put on the tire

5.

	Main Verb	Subject	Infinitive	Subject
a.	considered	I	be	the movie
b.	were	the men	finish	the men
c.	wants	Penny	play	the children
d.	asked	the manager	work	Jim
e.	is	to win a gold medal	win	every athlete
f.	lost	the team	play	the team
g.	should help	the Scout	cross	the old woman

6. a. 3
   b. 2, 5
   c. 9
   d. 10, 13, 5
   e. 11
   f. 7
   g. 12
   h. 4, 13, 5, 8
   i. 4, 1
   j. 8
   k. 2, 5
   l. 6

Exercise 41: Answers

1. a. (V_L / Adj / Adv) staying / healthy / after 60
   b. (V / NP^2 / Adv) riding / your bike / along the trail
   c. (V_i / Adv / Adv) exercising / at noon / every day
   d. (V_{be} / Adv / Adv) being / in the dark / all the time
   e. (V_L / NP^1 / Adv) remaining / friends / in spite of constant arguments
   f. (V / NP^2 / Adv) eating / three meals / every day

2. a. P
   b. PI
   c. P
   d. I
   e. P
   f. P
   g. —
   h. I
   i. —
   j. P
   k. PI

3. a. Mary
   b. the team
   c. Dad and Harry
   d. Both of the girls
   e. Nancy
   f. the children
   g. two boys

4. a. mowing our neighbors' lawns: OP
   b. Buying food for our family: S
   c. collecting shells at different beaches: PN
   d. His interning at County Hospital: S
   e. investing some money in gold coins: DO
   f. finding someone to take care of the children: PN
   g. Dad's working overtime: DO
   h. cleaning out the garage: OP

5. a. Andrea loves (something):
   Experiencer—process—complement,
   Andrea hike(s) in the mountains:
   Mover—action—location
   b. John exercises every day by (some means):
   Mover—action—frequency—manner,
   John run(s) around the mall:
   Mover—action—location

6. a. 4, 1, 6
   b. 2
   c. 7, 3, 7, 3
   d. 1, 7, 6, 7
   e. 4
   f. 3, 4
   g. 3
   h. 4, 3
   i. 4, 3
   j. 3, 4, 3
   k. 3, 3, 7, 3
   l. 4, 3
   m. 5, 3, 7, 3
   n. 3, 6, 7
   o. 3, 4, 4
   p. 2, 4

CHAPTER 19

Practice Test

1. Identify the voice or voice and aspect of the infinitive phrases.

	Voice	*Aspect*
a. to have found	__________	__________
b. to have been waiting	__________	__________
c. to laugh	__________	__________
d. to have been waived	__________	__________
e. to be returned	__________	__________
f. to be graduating	__________	__________

2. Analyze the constituents of the infinitive phrases by marking off and labeling them.

   a. to be friends

   b. to have been sitting down

   c. to be mysterious

   d. to have been in bed until noon

   e. to walk each evening

   f. to become quiet

   g. to pass out the papers

3. State the feature necessary in verbs so that they may have infinitives as complements.

   ____

   ____

4. Identify the object of the verb in each sentence as an infinitive phrase (IP), noun phrase + infinitive phrase (NP + IP), or accusative pronoun + inf phrase (AP + IP).

   a. Lisa should have told me to wait at the restaurant. ____________________

   b. Mr. Greeley may want him to work overtime. ____________________

c. We expected to eat on the patio. ______________________

d. That dog is always forcing our cat to climb a tree. ______________________

e. Harriet wanted to leave this morning. ______________________

5. Circle those verbs that may be followed immediately by infinitive complements with the same subject for both verbs.

a. proceed
b. strive
c. arrange
d. advise
e. remind
f. hasten
g. happen
h. praise
i. lead
j. aspire
k. propose
l. hear
m. postpone
n. promise

6. Write the propositions in the deep structure for each sentence and the semantic relationships for each proposition. Give the major proposition first.

a. Mother hates for Dad to read in bed.

______________________ : ______________________

______________________ : ______________________

b. The girls intended to chop the vegetables with the food processor.

______________________ : ______________________

______________________ : ______________________

c. Uncle Henry advised Jerry to become a lawyer.

______________________ : ______________________

______________________ : ______________________

7. Circle those verbs that require an NP different from the subject of the main verb as the subject of the infinitives.

a. watch
b. command
c. hear
d. direct
e. let
f. forbid
g. compel
h. decide
i. think
j. neglect
k. consent
l. urge
m. appear
n. try

8. Write the infinitive phrase in each sentence including the infinitive marker for each.

a. Janet let them sing in the show.

____

b. The players tried to make a triple play in the seventh inning.

____

c. Mary and Bob liked to eat at the restaurant where they first met.

____

d. Larry watched the boulder roll over the cliff.

____

e. Mother wanted the boys to go to the playground after school.

____

f. I heard the band play the school fight song.

____

9. Write the propositions and the semantic relationships of the propositions expressed in each sentence. Give the major proposition first.

   a. The plan must have been for Jane to cook the dinner.

   ____

   ____

   b. The man cut down a tree to have wood this winter.

   ____

   ____

   c. That movie is too grim for children to see.

   ____

   ____

10. Circle those adjectives that can have infinitive complements (without an intensifier to qualify the adjective).

a. silly	d. brave	g. ridiculous	j. dark
b. happy	e. sickly	h. early	
c. anxious	f. large	i. upset	

11. Underline the infinitive phrase and identify its function as direct object (NP^2), predicate nominative (NP^1), subject (NP^1), or adverbial of purpose (Adv).

    a. I like to read novels about the West. ______________________________

b. To remain on the basketball team, Jim practiced in the gym every afternoon. ____________________

c. To sit in the front row at the concert was very expensive. ____________________

d. Her goal was to graduate from college in three years. ____________________

e. His dog must have barked to scare the mailman. ____________________

12. Write the complete infinitive phrases contained in the sentences putting the deleted *to* in parentheses.

a. Sandra asked her secretary to come take dictation.

____

b. The movie made him want to be a Marine.

____

c. Dad is helping Mother learn to drive the car with a stick shift.

____

13. Identify the main verb, the subject of the main verb, the infinitive verb, and the subject of the infinitive.

a. The books were too difficult for the children to read.
b. The dog began to chase the bees.
c. Mary has a chance to study ballet in New York.
d. The upperclassmen made the pledges do their laundry.
e. The teacher told the child to wait for her mother.
f. Celia's dream was to live in New York.
g. Dad went to an exclusive shop to buy Mother's gift.

	Main Verb	*Subject*	*Infinitive*	*Subject*
a.				
b.				
c.				
d.				
e.				
f.				
g.				

14. Match the appropriate syntactic function(s) to the infinitive (phrase) in each sentence.

1. Inf compl, obj of verb
2. NP + inf compl
3. Accus pro + inf compl
4. for. . .to inf compl of *be*
5. NP + inf compl + del
6. Adj + inf compl
7. Inf compl (predicate nominative)
8. Inf phrase as subject
9. Inf compl of quasi-modal
10. Inf of purpose
11. Inf compl of NP
12. Passive inf
13. Deletion

a. To sail on the Chesapeake Bay is always a treat. ______________

b. Dad expects us to be home by midnight. ______________

c. The girls are driving to the beach to pick up some shells. ______________

d. The boys were hungry enough to eat a bear. ______________

e. The committee chair ought to stop the arguments. ______________

f. The baby likes to be bathed in the big bathtub. ______________

g. The plan to vacation in Hawaii was unrealistic. ______________

h. You can't make a chicken lay an egg. ______________

i. Our expectation was to arrive before dinner. ______________

j. Jack expects Martina to be elected. ______________

k. Did you watch the team swim the relay? ______________

15. Analyze the constituents in the participle phrases by marking off and labeling them.

a. entering a horse in a show

b. feeling free as a bird

c. being in a daze every morning

d. keeping trim through exercise

e. putting all your eggs in one basket

f. becoming a doctor after he was 50

16. Write (P) in the blank if the verb can be immediately followed by a participle only, (PI) if it can be followed by an infinitive or participle, (I) if only by an infinitive; leave blank if it can be followed by none of the above.

a. resume ____________ g. prescribe ____________

b. cease ____________ h. miss ____________

c. feel ____________ i. remember ____________

d. hesitate ____________ j. intend ____________

e. deny ____________ k. try ____________

f. think ____________

17. Write the subject of the embedded proposition in the blank.

a. His taking his students to the movies cost him too much money. ____________

b. "Your driving that van with bad tires worries me," Mother told Bill. ____________

c. Sally surprised her parents by earning enough money for her fall clothes. ____________

d. Playing with matches is dangerous. ____________

e. Mary congratulated Sue on her being elected to the Student Council. ____________

f. Uncle Jack got a ticket for driving with an expired license. ____________

g. The children were scolded by their teacher for throwing sand at one another. ____________

18. Identify the complete participle and infinitive nominalizations and identify the function as subject (S), direct object (DO), predicate nominative (PN), or object of a preposition (OP).

a. Sue's pet peeve is being teased by Jeff. ____________

b. By driving with no stops, we made the trip in one day. ____________

c. Swimming in such cold water gives me cramps. ____________

d. For going back and forth to work he is getting a motorcycle. ____________

e. Paula didn't remember meeting Tom at the beach last summer. ______________________

f. Her complaining about the food angered Mother. ______________________

g. I tried to stop his crying by picking him up. ______________________

h. Bob's intention was to immediately start dieting. ______________________

19. Identify the underlying propositions in the sentence and the semantic relationships for each.

a. The baby's crying always awakens Mother.

____

____

____

____

b. John hates washing the car.

____

____

____

____

20. Identify all the complexities in each of the sentences.

Modalities:
1. imperative
2. negation
3. yes-no question
4. *wh*-question

Conjoinings:
5. coordination
6. subordination

Elaborations:
7. poss det or noun
8. adj modifier or noun adjunct
9. relative clause
10. *-ing* participle modifier
11. *-en* participle modifier
12. prep phrase modifier
13. appositive
14. comparative
15. infinitive complement/nominalization
16. participle complement/nominalization

Transformations: 17. pronominal
18. reflex pro intens or reflex intens movt
19. adv preposing
20. intensifier
21. indirect obj preposing
22. *do*-support
23. contraction
24. aux or copula invers
25. prt movt
26. there
27. passive
28. deletion

a. Did the children expect something exciting to happen? (6) ____________________

b. Armand often goes to the library to get books to read when he's traveling. (6) ____________________

c. Sue wanted to do work that would help people; so she decided to become a doctor or a teacher. (8) ____________________

d. If Joe helps me clean the house we'll share the money I get and see a movie. (12) ____________________

e. Jim tried shaving himself with that blade, but it was too dull. (5) ____________________

f. Fishing and hiking are more relaxing for Josh than swimming. (7) ____________________

g. As the evening became cooler, people began to go in and get sweaters. (7) ____________________

h. The girl was afraid to leave the yard because she had been knocked down by a dog. (4) ____________________

i. The man painting our house is beginning to do the trim in the den, which will be the last room he paints. (9) ____________________

Chapter 19 Practice Test: Answers

1. a. perfect, active
   b. perfect progressive, active
   c. active
   d. perfect, passive
   e. passive
   f. progressive, active

2. a. (V_L / NP^1) to be / friends
   b. (V_i) to have been sitting down
   c. (V_L / Adj) to be / mysterious
   d. (V_{be} / Adv / Adv) to have been / in bed / until noon
   e. (V_i / Adv) to walk / each evening
   f. (V_L / Adj) to become / quiet
   g. (V / NP^2) to pass out / the papers

3. Catenation

4. a. AP + IP
   b. AP + IP
   c. IP
   d. NP + IP
   e. IP

5. a, b, c, f, g, j, k, n

6. a. Mother hate (something):
      Experiencer—process—complement,
      Dads read bed:
      Experiencer—process—location
   b. girl intend (something):
      Experiencer—process—complement,
      girl chop vegetable (with) processor:
      Agent—action—patient—instrument,
      processor be (for) food:
      Entity—stative—reason
   c. Uncle Henry advise (something):
      Agent—action—complement,
      Jerry become lawyer:
      Entity—stative—equivalent

7. a, b, c, d, e, f, g, l

8. a. (to) sing in the show
   b. to make a triple play (in the seventh inning)
   c. to eat at the restaurant where they first met
   d. (to) roll over the cliff
   e. to go to the playground after school
   f. (to) play the school fight song

9. a. plan be (something):
      Entity—stative—equivalent,
      Jane cook dinner:
      Experiencer—process—complement
   b. man cut down tree (for some reason):
      Agent—action—patient—reason,
      man have wood winter:
      Possessor—process—patient—time
   c. movie be (too) grim:
      Entity—stative—intensifier—quality,
      children see movie:
      Experiencer—process—complement

10. a, b, c, d, g

11. a. to read novels about the West, NP^2
    b. to remain on the basketball team, Adv
    c. to sit in the front row at the concert, NP^1
    d. to graduate from college in three years, NP^1
    e. to scare the mailman, Adv

12. a. to come take dictation,
       (to) take dictation
    b. (to) want to be a Marine,
       to be a Marine
    c. (to) learn to drive the car with a stick shift,
       to drive the car with a stick shift

13.

	Main Verb	*Subject*	*Infinitive*	*Subject*
a.	were	The books	read	the children
b.	began	The dog	chase	the dog
c.	has	Mary	study	Mary
d.	made	the upper-classmen	do	the pledges
e.	told	The teacher	wait	the child
f.	was	Celia's dream	live	Celia
g.	went	Dad	buy	Dad

14. a. 8
    b. 3
    c. 10
    d. 6
    e. 9
    f. 1, 12, 13
    g. 11
    h. 5
    i. 7
    j. 2, 12, 13
    k. 5, (13)

15. a. (V / NP^2 / Adv) entering / a horse / in a show
    b. (V_L / Adj) feeling / free as a bird
    c. (V_L / Adv / Adv) being / in a daze / every morning
    d. (V_L / Adj / Adv) keeping / trim / through exercise
    e. (V / NP^2 / Adv) putting / all your eggs / in one basket
    f. (V_L / NP^1 / Adv) becoming / a doctor / after he was 50

16. a. P
    b. PI
    c. —
    d. PI
    e. P
    f. —
    g. P
    h. P
    i. PI
    j. PI
    k. PI

17. a. He
    b. Bill
    c. Sally
    d. no subject given (anyone)
    e. Sue
    f. Uncle Jack
    g. the children

18. a. being teased by Jeff: PN
    b. driving with no stops: OP
    c. Swimming in such cold water: S
    d. going back and forth to work: OP
    e. meeting Tom at the beach last summer: DO
    f. Her complaining about the food: S
    g. to stop his crying: DO,
       his crying: DO, picking him up: OP
    h. to immediately start dieting: PN,
       dieting: DO

19. a. something awaken Mother always:
       Agent—process—patient—frequency,
       baby cry: Mover—action
    b. John hate something:
       Experiencer—process—complement,
       John wash car: Agent—action—patient

20. a. 22, 3, 24, 17, 10, 15
    b. 19, 15, 15, 6, 17, 23
    c. 15, 17, 9, 5, (6), 17, 15, 5, 28
    d. 6, 19, 17, 15, 28, 17, 23, 9, 28, 17, 5, 28
    e. 16, 17, 5, 17, 20
    f. 16, 16, 5, 28, 14, 28, 16
    g. 6, 19, 14, 15, 5, 28, 15
    h. 15, 6, 17, 27
    i 10, 7, 15, 12, 9, 17, 9, 17, 28

CHAPTER 20

Complementation with Direct and Indirect Discourse

Exercise 42

1. Analyze the sentences by marking off and labeling the constituents.

   a. "Let's go," said Marcia as she got into the car.

   b. That morning the teacher remarked, "There are more students absent every day."

   c. "Where are your mittens?" asked Mother when the children came in.

   d. Mary pretended to be hurt, and she exclaimed, "I can't walk because my ankle's broken!"

   e. When Dad said, "It's going to freeze," Mother went outside to bring in the plants.

2. List 5 verbs other than those used in the sentences above that may be used with direct discourse.

   ____

   ____

3. Identify the order of the subject (S), verb (V), direct object (DO), and indirect object (IO) in the sentences.

   a. "Clean up your room," Mother told Jim.

   ____

   b. "You are a good student," said the teacher.

   ____

   c. Jan said to the children, "I'll read you a story in a minute."

   ____

   d. "The cardinals are eating the seeds now," the old man said.

   ____

Exercise 43

1. Change the following sentences to indirect discourse, using the rule of attracted sequence of tense in the verbs.

   a. Mother told me, "You should iron your clothes now."

   ____

   ____

   b. The girls asked Tom, "Did you bring the cookies for the party?"

   ____

   ____

   c. Jerry asked Lucy, "How much money do you have?"

   ____

   ____

   d. The librarian told the children, "Please be quiet."

   ____

   ____

2. Analyze the sentences by marking off and labeling the constituents.

   a. When the teacher told her that she had failed the test, Mary began to cry.

   b. The conductor announced that the next stop was Fairlington.

   c. My mother hasn't said how many people are coming for dinner on Thanksgiving.

   d. Because Nan was angry, she said we should get out of the house.

   e. You may explain why you are late, but I don't want to hear that the car broke down.

3. List the pronouns that must be changed for the indirect discourse and state the change in person that is required.

   a. Nancy said to Bill, "I have $5, but you have only $3."

   ____

   b. The girls asked, "When can we leave?"

   ____

c. Joe told me, "You are lucky."

___

d. Dad said to us, "You can clean up the yard for me."

___

4. Label the following as action (A) or process (P) verbs.

a. consider ___ h. learn ___

b. whisper ___ i. remember ___

c. announce ___ j. profess ___

d. know ___ k. doubt ___

e. exclaim ___ l. believe ___

f. see ___ m. recognize ___

g. state ___ n. expect ___

5. Identify the embedded proposition as a statement, yes-no question, *wh*-question, or imperative.

a. All of the boys asked whether they could go swimming. ___

b. Mother admitted she was tired. ___

c. Did you learn how the game came out? ___

d. When will you understand that I can't always help you? ___

e. Did the driver tell you to get off the bus? ___

6. For each of the sentences, write the underlying propositions and give the semantic relationships expressed in each proposition. Give the major proposition first.

a. The girl screamed, "That boy kicked the dog!"

(1) ___

___

(2) ___

___

b. Elena promised that she would write a letter to Grandma.

(1) ___

___

(2) ______________________________

____

c. Dad noticed that Mother was upset.

(1) ______________________________

____

(2) ______________________________

____

d. The boys must have forgotten that they didn't put the car in the garage.

(1) ______________________________

____

(2) ______________________________

____

7. Underline the complement phrase or clause used as a noun (*that*) clause complement (NCC) of an action (A) or process (P) verb, an embedded yes-no (EQ yes-no) or *wh*-(EQ *wh*) complement of an action or process verb, a *wh*- + infinitive complement (*wh*- + inf), or an adjective plus noun clause complement (Adj + NCC).

a. The children didn't realize how far they had gone.

____

b. That student seems never to know when to keep quiet.

____

c. Are you sure that the meeting is in the gym?

____

d. Tom feels that he was innocent.

____

e. Jane wondered why Mary didn't talk to her.

____

f. Mother forgot whether she had turned off the iron.

____

g. Boris was happy that his dog wasn't hurt.

____

h. The police officer said that I was speeding.

____

i. The babysitter didn't know where the children were.

____

j. The girls were sorry Jim couldn't come to the party.

____

8. Identify only the listed complexities in each of the sentences.

Conjoinings:	1. adv cl of time, etc.
	2. conditional cl
Elaborations:	3. relative cl
	4. infinitive complement
	5. direct discourse
	6. *that* cl complement
	7. embedded *wh*-question
	8. embedded yes-no question
	9. *wh*- + inf complement
Transformations:	10. indirect obj preposing
	11. deletion

a. Larry found out the place where the group was going to pick apples. ____________

b. You'll have to decide if you want ice cream for dessert. ____________

c. Did you ask Mary how much she thinks the dress will cost? ____________

d. If you can tell me if all your cousins are coming to the picnic, I can figure out how many pounds of meat I should buy. ____________

e. Does Matt know where we can buy a horse? ____________

f. When will you learn that Mother needs some time that she can be alone? ____________

g. Adrienne must find out if she can go. ____________

h. Bill always thinks he knows how to do everything. ____________

i. Suselle was happy she could see you when you were here. ____________

j. Clint asked, "Where can we chop wood?" ____________

Exercise 42: Answers

NP^2 V NP^1 Adv
1. a. "Let's go," / said / Marcia / as she got into the car.

Adv NP^1 V NP^2
b. That morning / the teacher / remarked, / "There are more students absent every day."

NP^2 V NP^1 Adv
c. "Where are your mittens?" / asked / Mother / when the children came in.

NP^1 V NP^2 NP^1 V NP^2
d. Mary / pretended / to be hurt, / (and) she / exclaimed, / "I can't walk because my ankle's broken.

Adv NP V_i Adv Adv
e. When Dad said, "It's going to freeze," / Mother / went / outside / to bring in the plants.

2. These answers are only examples. Your answers may vary.
whisper, yell, murmur, cry, answer

3. a. DO + S + V + IO
b. DO + V + S
c. S + V + IO + DO
d. DO + S + V

Exercise 43: Answers

1. a. Mother told me that I should iron my clothes now.
b. The girls asked Tom if he brought the cookies for the party.
c. Jerry asked Lucy how much money she had.
d. The librarian told the children to please be quiet.

Adv NP^1 V NP^2
2. a. When the teacher told her that she had failed the test, / Mary / began / to cry.

NP^1 V NP^2
b. The conductor / announced / that the next stop was Fairlington.

NP^1 V NP^2
c. My mother / hasn't said / how many people are coming for Thanksgiving dinner.

Adv NP^1 V NP^2
d. Because Nan was angry, / she / said / we should get out of the house.

NP^1 V NP^2 NP^1 V NP^2
e. You / may explain / why you are late, / (but) / I / don't want / to hear that the car broke down.

3. a. I → she: 1st to 3rd person, you → he: 2nd to 3rd pers
b. We → they: 1st to 3rd pers
c. you → I: 2nd to 1st pers
d. you → we: 2nd to 1st pers, me → him: 1st to 3rd pers

4. a. P
   b. A
   c. A
   d. P
   e. A
   f. P
   g. A
   h. P
   i. P
   j. A
   k. P
   l. P
   m. P
   n. P

5. a. yes-no question
   b. statement
   c. *wh*-question
   d. statement
   e. imperative

6. a. the girl screamed (something):
   Agent—action—complement,
   that boy kicked the dog: Agent—action—patient
   b. Elena promised (something):
   Experiencer—process—complement,
   Elena will write a letter to Grandma:
   Agent—action—complement—recipient (beneficiary)
   c. Dad noticed (something):
   Experiencer—process—complement,
   Mother was upset: Entity—stative—condition
   d. the boys must have forgotten (something):
   Experiencer—process—complement,
   the boys (didn't) put the car in the garage:
   Agent—action—patient—location

7. a. how far they had gone, EQ *wh*-P
   b. when to keep quiet, *wh*- + inf
   c. that the meeting is in the gym, Adj + NCC
   d. that he was innocent, NCC-P
   e. why Mary didn't talk to her, EQ *wh*-P
   f. whether she had turned off the iron, EQ yes-no-P
   g. that his dog wasn't hurt, Adj + NCC
   h. that I was speeding, NCC-A
   i. where the children were, EQ *wh*-P
   j. (that) Jim couldn't come to the party, Adj + NCC

8. a. 3, 4
   b. 4, 8
   c. 10, 7, 6, 11
   d. 2, 10, 8, 7, 3, 11
   e. 7
   f. 6, 3
   g. 8
   h. 6, 11, 9
   i. 6, 11, 1
   j. 5

CHAPTER 20

Practice Test

1. Analyze the sentences by marking off and labeling the constituents.

   a. The mayor said, "All the clerks are busy now."

   b. "Where are your pencils?" the teacher asked.

   c. After they finished dinner, Tom said, "We should go to town for a sundae."

   d. "Don't put all your eggs in one basket," Jean remarked when Sally told her about Bill.

   e. Jill began to sing loudly, and Dad said, "Will you be quiet so I can work?"

2. List 10 action verbs other than those used in the sentences above that may be followed by direct discourse.

   ____

   ____

3. Identify the order of the subject (S), verb (V), direct object (DO), and indirect object (IO) in the sentences.

   a. The teacher said to the principal, "A lot of the children have the flu." ____________________

   b. "They went that way," the witness told the police officer. ____________________

   c. "The dog is limping a little," said the old man. ____________________

   d. "It's going to rain," said Mother, "so put on your boots. ____________________

4. Change the following sentences to indirect discourse, using the rule of attracted sequence of tense in the verbs.

   a. Larry asked Tim, "Why can't you help me?"

      ____

   b. The teacher told the twins, "Show me your nametags so I can tell which is which."

      ____

      ____

c. Martin asked Sally, "Do you have time to help me with my math?"

____

____

d. Grandmother hinted to me, "Your gift is something you can wear."

____

____

5. Analyze the sentences by marking off and labeling the constituents.

   a. Since he has been old enough to talk, Jack has said he wants to be a fire fighter.

   b. The young man loudly professed that he was right.

   c. With great exasperation, the supervisor told us to build a higher tower than that.

   d. Every day someone asks if we go to the gym after lunch.

   e. The nurse explained why the tests were necessary, but Jim said he didn't understand what she was saying.

6. List the changes that must be made for indirect discourse, indicating the pronouns and genitive determiners and the changes in person or case necessary.

   a. Larry told the girls, "I can carry the boxes for you."

   ____

   b. Mother asked us, "Where are you going?"

   ____

   c. Dad said to Betty, "You look beautiful in your dress."

   ____

   d. The teacher told them, "You may call me at home."

   ____

7. Label the following as action (A) or process (P) verbs.

a. announce	____________	e. ask	____________
b. scream	____________	f. worry	____________
c. find out	____________	g. inquire	____________
d. perceive	____________	h. recollect	____________

i. observe ____________ l. wish ____________

j. declare ____________ m. decide ____________

k. request ____________ n. desire ____________

8. Identify the embedded proposition as a statement, yes-no question, *wh*-question, or imperative.

   a. Do you remember how often we met last year? ____________

   b. The children suggested that the picnic should be at the lake. ____________

   c. When will you hear if Uncle Bill is coming? ____________

   d. Did you say to put in three cups of flour? ____________

   e. Why can't you remember where you leave your keys? ____________

9. For each of the sentences, write the underlying propositions and give the semantic relationships expressed in each proposition.

   a. The children sensed that the teacher was quite ill.

      (1) ____________

      ____

      (2) ____________

      ____

   b. Maureen said shyly, "You have beautiful eyes."

      (1) ____________

      ____

      (2) ____________

      ____

      (3) ____________

      ____

   c. Sally remembered that she had given the keys to Dad.

      (1) ____________

      ____

(2) ____

____

d. Paulino asserted that he loved Mariela.

(1) ____

____

(2) ____

____

10. Identify all the complexities in each sentence.

Modalities:
1. imperative
2. negation
3. yes-no question
4. *wh*-question

Conjoinings:
5. coordination
6. subordination

Elaborations:
7. poss det or noun
8. adj or noun adjunct modifier
9. relative clause
10. *-ing* participle modifier
11. *-en* participle modifier
12. prep phrase modifier
13. appositive
14. comparative
15. inf compl/nominal
16. part compl/nominal
17. direct discourse
18. *that* clause complement
19. embedded *wh*-question (*wh*-clause complement)
20. embedded yes-no question
21. *wh*- + infinitive complement

Transformations:
22. pronominal
23. reflex pro intens or intens movt
24. adv preposing
25. intensifier
26. ind obj preposing
27. *do*-support
28. contraction
29. aux or copula invers
30. prt movt
31. there
32. passive
33. deletion

a. When he arrived and saw what his daughter had done, he told her to go to bed. (11) ______________________

b. Nelson didn't know if the man would be very upset if the children took the dog out. (7) ______________________

c. All those children playing cards seem to really understand how that game should be played. (6) ______________________

d. We saw the movie you recommended and thought it was excellent. (9) ______________________

e. When the girls started talking about the older boys that they had dated, Tom and Jack decided to leave. (11) ______________________

f. Beth never discovered the solution to the hardest puzzle that Dad had, but she could solve all the easier puzzles. (10) ______________________

g. Arthur said, "Can Uncle Bill teach us the soccer rules this summer, or does he think we'll learn ourselves?" (16) ______________________

h. Jerry told Raul playing with matches was dangerous but Raul didn't listen to what he said and was badly burned. (15) ______________________

i. Mother will not know where to go when she gets to the school and finds that no one has waited to show her the way. (12) ______________________

Chapter 20 Practice Test: Answers

1. a. The mayor (NP1) / said, (V) / "All the clerks are busy now." (NP2)
   b. "Where are your pencils?" (NP2) / the teacher (NP1) / asked. (V)
   c. After they finished dinner (Adv) / Tom (NP1) / said, (V) / "We should go to town for a sundae. (NP2)
   d. "Don't put all your eggs in one basket," (NP2) / Jean (NP1) / remarked (V) / when Sally told her about Bill. (Adv)
   e. Jill (NP1) / began (V) / to sing loudly (NP2) / (and) / Dad (NP1) / said (V) / "Will you be quiet so I can work?" (NP2)

2. These answers are only examples. Your answers may vary.
   shout, cry, scream, yell, profess, call out, state, sing, gasp, assert

3. a. S + V + IO + DO
   b. DO + S + V + IO
   c. DO + V + S
   d. DO + V + S + DO

4. a. Larry asked Tim why he couldn't help him.
   b. The teacher told the twins to show her their nametags so she could tell which was which.
   c. Martin asked Sally if (whether) she had time to help him with his math.
   d. Grandmother hinted to me that my gift was something I could wear.

5. a. (Adv) Since he has been old enough to talk, / (NP1) Jack / (V) has said / (NP2) he wants to be a fire fighter.
   b. (NP1) The young man / (Adv) loudly / (V) professed / (NP2) that he was right.
   c. (Adv) With great exasperation / (NP1) the supervisor / (V) told / (pre IO) us / (NP2) to build a higher tower than that.
   d. (Adv) Every day / (NP1) someone / (V) asks / (NP2) if we go to the gym after lunch.
   e. (NP1) The nurse / (V) explained / (NP2) why the tests were necessary / (but) (NP1) Jim / (V) said / (NP2) he didn't understand what she was saying.

6. a. I → he: 1st to 3rd pers,
      you → them: 2nd to 3rd pers
   b. you → we: 2nd to 1st pers
   c. you → she: 2nd to 3rd pers,
      your → her: 2nd to 3rd pers
   d. you → they: 2nd to 3rd pers,
      me → her (him): 1st to 3rd pers

7. a. A
   b. A
   c. P
   d. P
   e. A
   f. P
   g. A
   h. P
   i. P
   j. A
   k. A
   l. P
   m. P
   n. P

8. a. *wh*-question
   b. statement
   c. yes-no question
   d. imperative
   e. *wh*-question

9. a. children sense (something):
      Experiencer—process—complement,
      teacher be (quite) ill:
      Entity—stative—intensifier—condition
   b. Maureen say (something) shyly:
      Agent—action—complement—manner,
      someone have eye: Entity—stative—part,
      eye be beautiful: Entity—stative—quality
   c. Sally remember (something):
      Experiencer—process—complement,
      Sally give key (to) Dad:
      Agent—action—patient—recipient
   d. Paulino assert (something):
      Agent—action—complement,
      Paulino love Mariela:
      Experiencer—process—patient

10. a. 6, 24, 22, 5, 33, 19, 7, 22, 26, 22, 15
    b. 27, 2, 28, 20, 25, 6, 30
    c. 10, 15, 24, 19, 32, 33
    d. 22, 9, 33, 22, 5, 33, 18, 33, 22
    e. 6, 24, 16, 8, 14, 9, 22, 22, 5, 33, 15
    f. 24, 2, 8, 14, 9, 22, 5, 22, 8, 14
    g. 17, 3, 29, 26, 22, 8, 5, 3, 27, 29, 22, 18, 33, 22, 28, 23
    h. 26, 18, 33, 16, 5, 27, 2, 28, 19, 22, 5, 33, 24, 32, 33
    i. 2, 21, 6, 22, 5, 33, 18, 22, 2, 15, 22, 26

CHAPTER 21

Complementation with *Wh*-Clauses, Factive Clauses, and Other Nominalizations

Exercise 44

1. Underline the *wh*-clause complements and identify each as a subject (S), direct object (DO), predicate nominative (PN), indirect object (IO), and/or object of a preposition (OP).

   a. What kind of candy do you have for whoever comes on Halloween? ________________

   b. The teacher must not have discovered what you put in her desk. ________________

   c. How Jane asks about having a party will influence Mother's decision. ________________

   d. Was that who you were expecting on the phone? ________________

   e. They will probably offer the job to whoever walks in the door. ________________

   f. The winner will be whoever reaches the finish line first without dropping the peanut. ________________

   g. They made a fire with whatever wood they could find in the yard. ________________

   h. The committee sends whoever contributes an Olympics pin. ________________

2. Underline and identify the *that* clauses that are subjects (S) or complements (C) of verbs.

   a. They gave a prize to the team that had the lowest score. ________________

   b. The problem was that Mary was sick the day of the party. ________________

   c. The girls understood that the boys had football practice. ________________

   d. They gave that student from New York a hard time. ________________

   e. That Dad has to work on Saturdays disturbs everyone in the family. ________________

3. Write the following sentences after applying the *it*-replacement and extraposition transformations.

   a. That no one liked the dessert must have upset the hostess.

   ____

   ____

   b. That the children had been playing in the mud should have been apparent.

   ____

   ____

Exercise 45

1. Underline the factive clauses in the sentences. Identify any other *that* clauses as relative clauses (RC) or noun clause complements (NCC).

   a. The problem that the coach foresaw was injury to one of the quarterbacks. ______________

   b. We understood his feeling that an injury could result in their losing the game. ______________

   c. He thinks, however, that injuries caused the team's losses this year. ______________

   d. He should remember the manager's warning that their defense was weak. ______________

   e. The worst thing that could happen is that the team couldn't be in the regional tournament. ______________

   f. The opinion of the alumni that the team should be in the tournament every year worries the coach. ______________

   g. The alumni may get the idea that the coach should be replaced. ______________

2. Apply the passive and extraposition transformations to those sentences with the appropriate factive clauses.

   a. One of the police officers made the statement that Mr. Smith started the fight.

   ____

   ____

   b. The decision of the judge that Mr. Smith pay a $500 fine was unjust.

   ____

   ____

c. Mr. Smith's lawyer will appeal the ruling that the judge made.

____

____

d. A local paper gave out the news that Mr. Smith would not appeal the decision.

____

____

3. State the propositions and semantic relationships expressed in the sentences.

a. The report that the scientists had discovered a cure was false.

(1) ____

____

(2) ____

____

b. Donna can give the candy to whoever is in class today.

(1) ____

____

(2) ____

____

c. Bill knew that Tom had pushed Sally.

(1) ____

____

(2) ____

____

4. Underline the nominalizations in each of the sentences.

a. All of the townspeople were horrified by the crash of the plane.

b. The explosion of the gas tank destroyed the house.

c. The inspector's rejection of the place did not upset any of the boys.

d. Were you disturbed by the howling of the wolves near the campsite?

e. None of us heard the shouts of the lost child.

5. State the propositions and the semantic relationships expressed in the sentences.

   a. The shriek of the teacher was heard by the principal.

   ____

   ____

   ____

   ____

   b. The development of the vaccine by Salk was a boon.

   ____

   ____

   ____

   ____

   c. The committee didn't like the woman's singing of the anthem.

   ____

   ____

   ____

   ____

   d. The psychologist observed the child's destruction of the toys.

   ____

   ____

   ____

   ____

6. Identify the listed complexities in each of the sentences.

Elaborations:	1. relative clause
	2. *that* clause compl/nominal
	3. *wh*-clause compl/nominal
	4. factive clause
	5. other nominalizations
Transformations:	6. passive
	7. deletion
	8. *it*-replacement
	9. extraposition

a. Mother said she'll love whatever you select. ____________________

b. They said that the movie they saw last weekend was terrible. ____________________

c. All of the children observed the raising of the flag that morning. ____________________

d. Mary laughed at Bill's proposal that she should go to the prom with Ed. ____________________

e. The reason that John gave didn't satisfy Dad. ____________________

f. Did Jim ask how Grandmother was doing? ____________________

g. It really upset everyone that the exam was canceled. ____________________

h. John made a guess that the bottle contained 1,567 beans. ____________________

i. It's a problem that the coach doesn't have enough players this season. ____________________

j. Georgia intimated that those boys take out whoever will go out with them. ____________________

k. The fact that we are having warm weather now portends that the winter will be severe. ____________________

l. The discovery of new clues by the Vice Squad resulted in the reopening of the case by the Chief Investigator. ____________________

m. The rule was proposed that only full-time students could vote in the election. ____________________

Exercise 44: Answers

1. a. whoever comes on Halloween, OP
   b. what you put in her desk, DO
   c. How Jane asks about having a party, S
   d. who you were expecting, PN
   e. whoever walks in the door, IO and OP
   f. whoever reaches the finish line first without dropping the peanut, PN
   g. whatever wood they could find near the house, OP
   h. whoever contributes, IO

2. a. (relative clause, does not apply)
   b. that Mary was sick the day of the party, C
   c. that the boys had football practice, C
   d. (demonstrative determiner, does not apply)
   e. That Dad has to work on Saturdays, S

3. a. It must have upset the hostess that no one liked the dessert.
   b. It should have been apparent that the children had been playing in the mud.

Exercise 45: Answers

1. a. that the coach foresaw, RC
   b. that an injury could result in their losing the game, FC
   c. that injuries caused the team's losses this year, NCC
   d. that their defense was weak, FC
   e. that could happen, RC, that the team couldn't be in the regional tournament, NCC
   f. that the team should be in the tournament every year, FC
   g. that the coach should be replaced, FC

2. a. The statement was made by one of the police officers that Mr. Smith had started the fight.
   b. not applicable, factive clause not complement of DO
   c. not applicable, relative clause
   d. The news was given out by a local paper that Mr. Smith would not appeal the decision.

3. a. report be false: Entity—stative—quality, scientist discover cure: Experiencer—process—complement
   b. Donna give candy (to) (someone): Agent—action—patient—recipient, (someone) be in class today: Entity—stative—location—time
   c. Bill know something: Experiencer—process—complement, Tom push Sally: Agent—action—patient

4. a. the crash of the plane
   b. the explosion of the gas tank
   c. the inspector's rejection of the place
   d. the howling of the wolves near the campsite
   e. the shouts of the lost child

5. a. principal hear something: Experiencer—process—complement, teacher shriek: Mover—action
   b. (something) be boon: Entity—stative—equivalent, Salk develop vaccine: Experiencer—process—complement
   c. committee like (something): Experiencer—process—complement, woman sing anthem: Agent—action—complement
   d. psychologist observe (something): Experiencer—process—complement, child destroy toy: Agent—action—patient

6. a. 2, 7, 3
   b. 2, 7, 1
   c. 5
   d. 5, 4
   e. 1
   f. 3
   g. 2, 8, 9, 6, 7
   h. 4
   i. 2, 8, 9
   j. 2, 3
   k. 4, 2
   l. 5, 5
   m. 4, 6, 7, 9

Chapter 21

Practice Test

1. Underline the *wh*-clauses and identify each as a subject (S), direct object (DO), predicate nominative (PN), indirect object (IO), and/or object of a preposition (OP).

   a. The girls didn't hear where the party would be.

   b. Whatever Mary makes for dessert will be good.

   c. Did you see who went into the house?

   d. Where is he going with whatever he has there?

   e. The treat must be whatever kind of candy is in the house.

   f. They mailed whoever responded to the questionnaire the results of the study.

   g. What Mother said went in one ear and out the other.

   h. Do you know what the prize will be?

   i. That woman tells her life story to whoever will listen.

2. Underline and identify the *that* clauses that are subjects (S) or complements (C) of verbs.

   a. That Jean was ill seemed apparent. ______________________

   b. No one knows that John is coming. ______________________

   c. Did they pick up that girl lying in the street? ______________________

   d. Everyone that came to the dance complained that there were no refreshments. ______________________

   e. That Sue was elected as president satisfied all the students. ______________________

   f. No one has located the book that you say that you lost. ______________________

3. Write the following sentences after applying the *it*-replacement and extraposition transformations.

   a. To tell a lie is a sin.

   ____

b. That the river was rising so fast scared the people.

c. That avocadoes grow on tall trees was surprising to me.

d. That Sally weighs 250 pounds is true.

4. Underline the factive clauses (FC) in the sentences. Identify any other *that* clauses as relatives (RC) or noun clause complements (NCC).

   a. The announcement that the ballet was canceled was made last week.

   b. The representative that made the announcement said that we could get refunds for our tickets.

   c. Then the news came out that another ballet was scheduled as a replacement.

   d. We didn't like the fact that it was not an international company.

   e. Some people must not have heard that another ballet was scheduled.

   f. The supposition that the company's dissatisfaction is only about their pay is not true.

   g. It was interesting that one of the stars left the company.

   h. A rumor was circulated that she received a better offer from another company.

5. Apply the passive and extraposition transformations to those sentences with the appropriate factive clauses.

   a. A student sent out an announcement that classes would be canceled on Friday.

   b. None of the teachers received the announcement that was sent out.

c. The realization that no students were coming to classes made someone call the principal's office.

____

____

d. The principal made a ruling that the day must be made up before the end of the year.

____

____

6. State the propositions and semantic relationships expressed in the sentences.

   a. The news that the panda was pregnant was announced by a veterinarian.

      (1) ______________________________

      ____

      (2) ______________________________

      ____

   b. Mother can't understand why Dad is so fat.

      (1) ______________________________

      ____

      (2) ______________________________

      ____

   c. The children can buy what they want.

      (1) ______________________________

      ____

      (2) ______________________________

      ____

7. Underline nominalizations with *of* in the sentences.

   a. The pulling of his teeth has made Dad ill.

   b. All of the people were interested in the raising of the Titanic.

   c. You could hear the whispers of the girls wherever you were in the room.

d. Mary's refusal of the candy surprised Mother.

e. They were crying about the disappearance of their rabbit.

8. Identify all the complexities in each sentence using the numbered list.

Modalities:	1. imperative
	2. negation
	3. yes-no question
	4. *wh*-question
Conjoinings:	5. coordination
	6. subordination
Elaborations:	7. poss det or noun
	8. adj modifier or noun adjunct
	9. relative clause
	10. *-ing* participle modifier
	11. *-en* participle modifier
	12. prep phrase modifier
	13. appositive
	14. comparative
	15. inf compl/nominal
	16. part compl/nominal
	17. direct discourse
	18. *that* cl compl
	19. *wh*-clause complement
	20. embedded yes-no question
	21. *wh*- + infinitive complement
	22. factive clause
	23. nominalized verb + *of* phrase
Transformations:	24. pronominal
	25. reflex pro intens or intens movt
	26. adv preposing
	27. intensifier
	28. ind obj preposing
	29. *do*-support
	30. contraction
	31. aux or copula invers
	32. prt movt
	33. there
	34. passive
	35. deletion
	36. *it*-replacement
	37. extraposition

a. Do you understand how that dog sleeps so soundly? (6) ____________________

b. The news that the hostages would be released made everyone happy. (6) ____________________

c. Cleaning the house is the most strenuous exercise that Mother gets, but she keeps her figure. (8) ________________

d. It is necessary that you renew the dog's license every year. (5) ________________

e. The children leaving on the bus knew that something was wrong and started crying. (6) ________________

f. A law was passed by the government that exceptional children should be educated in the mainstream. (6) ________________

g. The young man Tom hit didn't realize that Tom was disturbed by his wife's rejection of him. (12) ________________

h. The girls finally saw that they had to plan the dinner party themselves if they wanted to have it. (10) ________________

i. The claim was made by the clients that the fire had started when he was at the party. (5) ________________

j. Mother heard the wild shriek of some woman and rushed out of the house, carrying the baby in her arms. (6) ________________

k. Jerry told Jack, "This car runs more smoothly than mine, but it's too small for a large family." (10) ________________

l. The report that the thief had been apprehended made the people in the neighborhood feel safer. (7) ________________

m. Because Mary never bothers to tell Mother what time she'll be home, Mother sits around and worries. (11) ________________

n. How can they expect us to know it's a county ordinance here that a dog must be kept on a leash? (14) ________________

o. Which road you take at the fork determines whether you are going to the house or the barn. (6) ________________

9. Write the propositions and semantic relationships expressed in the sentences.

a. Flo didn't see the smirks of the girls.

____

____

____

____

b. The removal of the leaves by the city is slow this year.

c. Dad didn't believe Grant's explanation of the accident.

d. The faculty rejected the committee's revision of the by-laws.

Chapter 21 Practice Test: Answers

1. a. where the party would be, DO
   b. Whatever Mary makes for dessert, S
   c. who went into the house, DO
   d. whatever he has there, OP
   e. whatever kind of candy is in the house, PN
   f. whoever responded to the questionnaire, IO
   g. what Mother said, S
   h. what the prize will be, DO
   i. whoever will listen, IO and OP

2. a. That Jean was ill, S
   b. that John is coming, C
   c. no *that* clause complement
   d. that there were no refreshments, C
   e. that Sue was elected as president, S
   f. that you lost, C

3. a. It is a sin to tell a lie.
   b. It scared the people that the river was rising so fast.
   c. It was surprising to me that avocadoes grow on tall trees.
   d. It is true that Sally weighs 250 pounds.

4. a. that the ballet was canceled, FC
   b. that made the announcement, RC
      that we could get refunds for our tickets, NCC
   c. that another ballet was scheduled as a replacement, FC
   d. that it was not an international company, FC
   e. that another ballet was scheduled, NCC
   f. that the company's dissatisfaction is only about their pay, FC
   g. that one of the stars left the company, NCC
   h. that she received a better offer from another company, FC

5. a. An announcement was sent out by a student that classes would be canceled on Friday.
   b. not applicable because of rel cl
   c. not applicable, fact cl in subj
   d. A ruling was made by the principal that the day must be made up before the end of the year.

6. a. a veterinarian announced the news:
      Agent—action—complement,
      the panda was pregnant:
      Entity—stative—condition
   b. Mother understand something:
      Experiencer—process—complement,
      Dad is so fat (for some reason):
      Entity—stative—intensifier—condition—reason
   c. the children buy something:
      Agent—action—complement,
      the children want (something):
      Experiencer—process—complement

7. a. The pulling of his teeth
   b. the raising of the Titanic
   c. the whispers of the girls
   d. Mary's refusal of the candy
   e. the disappearance of their rabbit

8. a. 3, 29, 31, 24, 19, 27
   b. 22, 34, 35, 24, 15, 35
   c. 16, 14, 8, 9, 24, 5, 24, 7
   d. 36, 18, 37, 24, 7
   e. 10, 18, 24, 5, 35, 16
   f. 34, 22, 37, 8, 34, 35
   g. 8, 9, 35, 29, 2, 30, 18, 34, 7, 7, 23, 24
   h. 26, 18, 24, 15, 8, 25, 6, 24, 15, 24
   i. 34, 22, 37, 6, 24
   j. 8, 23, 5, 35, 10, 7
   k. 28, 17, 14, 24, 35, 5, 24, 30, 27, 8
   l. 22, 34, 35, 12, 15, 35, 14
   m. 26, 6, 26, 2, 15, 28, 19, 24, 30, 5, 35
   n. 4, 31, 24, 24, 15, 18, 35, 36, 30, 8, 22, 37, 34, 35
   o. 19, 24, 20, 24, 5, 35

9. a. Flo see (something):
      Experiencer—process—complement,
      girl smirk: Mover—action
   b. something be slow year:
      Entity—stative—condition—time,
      city remove leaf:
      Agent—action—patient
   c. Dad believe something:
      Experiencer—process—complement,
      Grant explain accident:
      Agent—action—complement
   d. faculty reject something:
      Experiencer—process—complement,
      committee revise by-law:
      Experiencer—process—complement

CHAPTER 22
Language Analysis IV Exercise

Complete both syntactic and semantic descriptions and summaries of the following sample.

Syntactic Description

1. Dad made Mother drive Tom to the dance because he says Tom's too young to drive at night.

   Sentence Pattern:

   Conjoinings:

   Elaborations:

   Transformations:

2. Did the boys like the idea the girls had that the class should surprise Mary by giving her a gift before she moves to Chicago?

   Sentence Pattern:

   Modalities:

   Conjoinings:

   Elaborations:

   Transformations:

3. The teacher of a class in the third grade was hit by a car this morning when she was driving to school, and now she's in the hospital.

   Sentence Patterns:

   Conjoinings:

   Elaborations:

   Transformations:

4. Our principal said running in the halls and not being polite were bad habits that the kids in the class have to change.

   Sentence Pattern:

   Modalities:

   Conjoinings:

   Elaborations:

   Transformations:

5. Mary knows where the store is, but she's afraid to walk there by herself because it's so dark now.

   Sentence Patterns:

   Conjoinings:

Elaborations:

Transformations:

Syntactic Summary

Sentence patterns	*Frequency of Occurrence*	*Comments*
intransitive verb	______	______
transitive verb	______	______
linking verb	______	______
Modalities		
negation	______	______
yes-no question	______	______
Conjoinings		
coordination	______	______
subordination	______	______
Elaborations		
possessive det or noun	______	______
adjective modifier	______	______
relative clause	______	______
prep phrase modifier	______	______
infinitive compl/nominal	______	______
participle compl/nominal	______	______
that clause complement	______	______
embedded question	______	______
factive clause	______	______
nominalized verb + *of* phrase	______	______
Transformations		
pronominalization	______	______
adverbial preposing	______	______
intensifier	______	______
indirect object preposing	______	______
auxiliary or copula inversion	______	______
do-support	______	______
contraction	______	______
passive	______	______
deletion	______	______
it-replacement	______	______

Semantic Description

1. Dad made Mother drive Tom to the dance because he says Tom's too young to drive at night.

   a. ______________________________

   ____

   b. ______________________________

   ____

   c. ______________________________

   ____

   d. ______________________________

   ____

   e. ______________________________

   ____

2. Did the boys like the idea the girls had that the class should surprise Mary by giving her a gift before she moves to Chicago?

   a. ______________________________

   ____

   b. ______________________________

   ____

   c. ______________________________

   ____

   d. ______________________________

   ____

   e. ______________________________

   ____

3. The teacher of a class in the third grade was hit by a car this morning when she was driving to school, and now she's in the hospital.

   a. ______________________________

   ____

   b. ______________________________

   ____

   c. ______________________________

   ____

   d. ______________________________

   ____

   e. ______________________________

   ____

4. Our principal said running in the halls and not being polite were bad habits that the kids in the class have to change.

   a. ______________________________

   ____

   b. ______________________________

   ____

   c. ______________________________

   ____

   d. ______________________________

   ____

   e. ______________________________

   ____

   f. ______________________________

   ____

   g. ______________________________

   ____

h. ____

____

5. Mary knows where the store is, but she's afraid to walk there by herself because it's so dark now.

a. ____

____

b. ____

____

c. ____

____

d. ____

____

e. ____

____

Semantic Summary

Number of utterances:
Number of propositions:
Propositions per utterance:

Noun cases	*Frequency of Occurrence*
Mover	________
Agent	________
Patient	________
Experiencer	________
Complement	________
Beneficiary (Recipient)	________
Possessor	________
Entity	________
Equivalent	________
Instrument	________
Verb cases	
Action	________
Process	________
Stative	________

Adverbial cases	*Frequency of Occurrence*
Location	________
Time	________
Manner	________
Reason	________
Intensifier	________
Attribute cases	
Quality	________
Condition	________
Ordinal	________
Age	________

Language Analysis IV Exercise: Answers

Syntactic Description

1. Sentence Pattern:	transitive verb
Conjoinings:	subordination (causal clause)
Elaborations:	infinitive complement
	that clause complement (of verb *say*)
	infinitive complement (of adj + intens)
Transformations:	personal pronominal
	deletion (*to* and *that*)
	contraction
	intensifier

2. Sentence Pattern:	transitive verb
Modalities:	yes-no question
Conjoinings:	subordination (adv cl time)
Elaborations:	relative clause
	factive clause
	participle compl
Transformations:	*do*-support
	aux invers
	deletion (rel pro)
	ind obj preposing
	pers pronominal (2)

3. Sentence Patterns:	transitive verb
	linking verb
Conjoinings:	coordination (conjunction)
Elaborations:	nomin verb + *of*
	prep phrase modifier
	relative adverb clause
Transformations:	passive
	pers pronominal (2)
	adv preposing
	contraction

4. Sentence Pattern:	transitive verb
Modalities:	negation
Conjoinings:	coordination (conjunction)
Elaborations:	poss det modifier
	participle nominal (2)
	adj modifier
	relative clause
	prep phr modifier
	infinitive compl
	that clause compl
Transformations:	deletion (*that* complementizer)
	relative pronominal

5. Sentence Patterns:	transitive verb
	linking verb
Conjoinings:	coordination (disjunction)
	subordination (causal cl)
Elaborations:	*wh*-clause complement
	inf compl (of adj)
Transformations:	pers pronominal
	contraction
	reflex pronomin
	it-replacement
	contraction
	intensifier

Syntactic Summary

Sentences	*Frequency of Occurrence*	*Comments*
transitive verb	5	
linking verb	2	
Modalities		
negation	1	with not
yes-no question	1	
Conjoinings		
coordination	3	conjunction, disjunction
subordination	3	causal, adverbial of time
Elaborations		
poss det or noun	1	our
adj modifier	1	
relative clause	3	rel pro + rel adv
prep phrase modifier	2	
inf compl/nominal	4	1 quasi-modal
participle compl/nominal	3	phrase with complement obj of verb *say*
that cl complement	2	
wh-clause complement	1	object of process verb
factive clause	1	
nominalized verb + *of* phr	1	-*er* nominal of V
Transformations		
pronominalization	8	personal, reflexive, relative
adverbial preposing	1	
intensifier	2	
indirect object preposing	1	
aux or copula inversion	1	
do-support	1	
contraction	4	N and pers pro + copula
passive	1	nontruncated, irreversible
deletion	5	
it-replacement	1	

Semantic Description

1. a. Dad make (something) (for some reason)
   Experiencer—process—complement—reason
   b. Mother drive Tom (to) dance
   Agent—action—patient—location
   c. Dad say something
   Agent—action—complement
   d. Tom be too young
   Entity—stative—intensifier—age
   e. Tom drive (at) night
   Mover—action—time

2. a. boy like idea
   Experiencer—process—complement
   b. girl have idea
   Experiencer—process—complement
   c. class surprise Mary (somehow) (sometime)
   Experiencer—process—beneficiary—manner—time
   d. class give gift (to) Mary
   Agent—action—patient—recipient
   e. Mary move (to) Chicago
   Mover—action—location

3. a. car hit teacher morning
   Instrument—action—patient—time
   b. (someone) teach class
   Experiencer—process—patient (beneficiary)
   c. class be (in) third grade
   Entity—stative—ordinal—location
   d. someone drive (to) work morning
   Mover—action—location—time
   someone teach
   Experiencer—process
   e. someone be (in) hospital now
   Entity—stative—location—time
   someone teach
   Experiencer—process

4. a. principal say (something)
   Agent—action—complement
   b. (someone) have principal
   Possessor—process—patient
   c. something be habit
   Entity—stative—equivalent
   d. kid run (in) hall
   Mover—action—location
   e. kid be polite
   Entity—stative—quality
   f. habit be bad
   Entity—stative—quality
   g. kid change habit
   Experiencer—process
   h. kid be (in) class
   Entity—stative—location

5. a. Mary know (something)
   Experiencer—process—complement
   b. store be somewhere
   Entity—stative—location
   c. Mary be afraid (for some reason)
   Entity—stative—condition—reason
   d. Mary walk there (by) Mary
   Mover—action—location—manner
   e. something be so dark now
   Entity—stative—intensifier—condition—time

Semantic Summary

Number of utterances:	5
Number of propositions:	28 or 29
Number of propositions per utterance:	5.6 or 5.9

Noun cases	*Frequency of Occurrence*
Mover	5
Agent	4
Patient	5
Experiencer	7
Complement	6
Beneficiary (Recipient)	2
Possessor	1
Entity	11
Equivalent	1
Instrument	1
Verb cases	
Action	10
Process	8
Stative	10

Adverbial cases	*Frequency of Occurrence*
Location	9
Time	6
Manner	2
Reason	2
Intensifier	2
Attribute cases	
Quality	2
Condition	2
Ordinal	1
Age	1

CHAPTERS 1–22

Review Test

1. Analyze the sentences by marking off and labeling the constituents.

   a. My brother who's a doctor on Park Avenue said that he has many patients coming to him from the west side.

   b. Before leaving for the beach, all of us should try to put everything on the walk near the car because it's easier to pack the car that way.

   c. The dream that we would vacation in Mexico City is finally becoming a reality.

   d. Whatever Jack did disturbed Mother so much that she didn't sleep for a week.

   e. If you tell Dad what you want he can get it for you tomorrow when he's in the city.

   f. A little girl sitting in the front row yelled that Bill broke the pencil she'd just sharpened.

   g. The call of the Canadian geese was so loud that all the children looked up.

   h. The news that Jim is being married in April was in Jane's letter.

   i. Whatever money Karen earns disappears quickly because she buys so many clothes.

   j. Biting her nails is a bad habit that Jean picked up when she was in college.

   k. The sound of a bitter wind on a snowy day doesn't seem bad when you're sitting in front of a warm fire.

2. Underline and identify the subjects (S), direct objects (DO), indirect objects (IO), and predicate nominatives (PN) in the sentences.

   a. The girl that he is dating said she's thinking of dropping him.

   b. This morning a boy in the back row announced to everybody in the class that he was going to be sick.

   c. The announcement that school would close at noon was a surprise that the students hadn't expected.

   d. That old man who sits in the yard will tell stories about his childhood to whoever will listen.

   e. The crash of a plane in the mountains may have been the tragedy the people were discussing in the drugstore this morning.

3. Identify the italicized words using the numbered list.

   1. participle nominalization
   2. participle phrase modifier
   3. infinitive introducer
   4. subordinating conjunction
   5. clause complementizer
   6. relative pronoun
   7. none of the above

   a. *If* you go, I will. ____________________

   b. I'll see *if* I can go. ____________________

   c. Mary ran *so* fast *that* she tripped. ____________________

   d. Mother gave me the book *that* she read. ____________________

   e. Jenna will find out *where* the movie is. ____________________

   f. Put the keys *where* I can find them. ____________________

   g. The thought *that* I would fail was always with me. ____________________

   h. Go *to* the store for me. ____________________

   i. Exercise *to* prolong your life. ____________________

   j. Linda is *sailing* her new boat today. ____________________

   k. I'll leave *so* you can go to bed. ____________________

   l. Terri made John (________) help her. ____________________

   m. Mother worries about Jane's *sailing* around the bay. ____________________

   n. Bill bought the car (________) Jack's *selling*. ____________________

   o. I'll see *whether* the train's coming. ____________________

   p. Leon's favorite sport is *swimming*. ____________________

   q. We heard (________) Jack was here. ____________________

   r. We saw Darla *sailing* around the bay. ____________________

4. Read the paragraphs and fill in the blanks.

Daedalus decided to make wings for himself and Icarus. He told Icarus to bring all the feathers he could find. With the feathers and with thread and wax Daedalus began to make the wings.

The day the wings were finished, there was a bright sun, a clear sky, and good winds. Before Icarus and Daedalus tried to escape, Daedalus reminded his son that they could not fly too low—for if they flew too close to the water, their wings would become wet and heavy from the waves of the sea.

("The Story of Daedalus and Icarus," 1971, pp. 37-38)

a. the first relative clause in the passage

____

b. two complements in indirect discourse, an imperative, and a statement

(1) ______________________________

(2) ______________________________

c. the types of transformations in the second sentence

(1) ______________________________

(2) ______________________________

(3) ______________________________

d. the first preposed adverbial clause and a conditional clause

(1) ______________________________

(2) ______________________________

e. the propositions underlying the surface structures of the first sentence in the first paragraph

(1) ______________________________

(2) ______________________________

(3) ______________________________

f. the specific kinds of complexities in the first part of the last sentence (before —)

(1) ______________ (7) ______________

(2) ______________ (8) ______________

(3) ______________ (9) ______________

(4) ______________ (10) ______________

(5) ______________ (11) ______________

(6) ______________

g. the specific types of conjoining in the last part of the second paragraph (after —)

(1) ______________________________

(2) ______________________________

(3) ______________________________

5. Identify all the complexities in each sentence using the numbered list.

Modalities:	1. imperative
	2. negation
	3. yes-no question
	4. *wh*-question
Conjoinings:	5. coordination
	6. subordination
Elaborations:	7. poss det or noun
	8. adj modifier or noun adjunct
	9. relative clause
	10. *-ing* participle modif
	11. *-en* participle modif
	12. prep phr modif
	13. appositive
	14. comparative
	15. inf compl/nominal
	16. part compl/nominal
	17. direct discourse
	18. *that* cl compl
	19. *wh*-clause complement
	20. embedded yes-no question
	21. *wh-* + inf compl
	22. factive clause
	23. nominal verb + *of* phrase
Transformations:	24. pronominal
	25. reflex pro intens or intens movt
	26. adv preposing
	27. intensifier
	28. ind obj preposing
	29. *do*-support
	30. contraction
	31. aux or copula invers
	32. prt movt
	33. there
	34. passive
	35. deletion
	36. *it*-replacement
	37. extraposition

a. Jeff never seems to realize what's going on behind his back; however, he sometimes acts paranoid. (9)

____

b. When does Mary think Brad will tell her who he's bringing to the dance at the club? (11)

____

c. The clerk was annoyed by the girls since she was sure that they wouldn't buy anything and that she was wasting her time waiting on them. (15)

____

d. When you finish working, clear the table off and don't forget to wash out those brushes you're using. (16)

____

e. The roar of the lion startled the children, but they were fascinated by the way he paced around the cage. (7)

____

f. If John finds out the reunion is in Arizona, he'll ask his boss if he can have the money to get there. (11)

____

g. It is strange that the college used less electricity this year than last, but that the bills were a lot higher than before. (11)

____

6. Complete syntactic and semantic descriptions of the following. In the semantic description give both the propositions and the semantic relationships.

Syntactic Description

a. One girl in the class thinks she's so smart that she never has to study.

Sentence Pattern:

Modalities:

Elaborations:

Transformations:

b. When you were little, did you know who was president?

Sentence Pattern:

Modalities:

Conjoinings:

Elaborations:

Transformations:

c. Mother was upset because of Nancy's staying home, and she went to her room to see how she was feeling.

Sentence Pattern:

Conjoinings:

Elaborations:

Transformations:

Semantic Description

a. (1) ______________________________

____

(2) ______________________________

____

(3) ______________________________

____

(4) ______________________________

____

b. (1) ______________________________

____

(2) ______________________________

____

(3) ______________________________

____

c. (1) ______________________________

____

(2) ______________________________

____

(3) ______________________________

____

(4) ______________________________

____

(5) ______________________________

____

(6) ______________________________

____

Chapters 1 – 22 Review Test: Answers

NP1 V NP2
1. a. My brother who's a doctor on Park Avenue / said / that he has many patients coming to him from the west side.

Adv NP1 V NP2
b. Before leaving for the beach / all of us / should try / to put everything on the walk near the car /

Adv
because it's easier to pack the car that way.

NP1 V_L Adv V_L NP1
c. The dream that we would vacation in Mexico City / is / finally / becoming / a reality.

NP1 V NP2 Adv
d. Whatever Jack did / disturbed / Mother / so much that she didn't sleep for a week.

Adv NP^1 V NP^2 Adv Adv
e. If you tell Dad what you want / he / can get / it / for you / tomorrow when he's in the city.

NP^1 V NP^2
f. A little girl sitting in the front row / yelled / that Bill broke the pencil she'd just sharpened.

NP V_L Adj
g. The call of the Canadian geese / was / so loud that all the children looked up.

NP^1 V_{be} Adv
h. The news that Jim is being married in April / was / in Jane's letter.

NP V_i Adv Adv
i. Whatever money Karen earns / disappears / quickly / because she buys so many clothes.

NP^1 V_L NP^1
j. Biting her nails / is / a bad habit that Jean picked up when she was in college.

NP V_L Adj Adv
k. The sound of a bitter wind on a snowy day / doesn't seem / bad / when you're sitting in front of a warm fire.

2. a. The girl that he is dating: S,
(that) she's thinking of dropping him: DO
b. a boy in the back row: S,
everybody in the class: IO,
that he was going to be sick: DO
c. The announcement that school would close at noon: S,
a surprise that the students hadn't expected: PN
d. That old man who sits in the yard: S,
stories about his childhood: DO,
whoever will listen: IO
e. The crash of a plane in the mountains: S,
the tragedy the people were discussing in the drugstore this morning: PN

3. a. 4
b. 5
c. 7, 5
d. 6
e. 5
f. 4
g. 5
h. 7
i. 3
j. 7
k. 4
l. 3
m. 1
n. 6, 7
o. 5
p. 1
q. 5
r. 2

4. a. (that) he could find
b. (1) to bring all the feathers he could find
(2) that they could not fly too low—for if they. .
c. (1) personal pronominalization
(2) indirect object preposing
(3) deletion
d. (1) Before Icarus and Daedalus tried to escape
(2) if they flew too close to the water
e. (1) Daedalus decided something
(2) Daedalus make wings for Daedalus
(3) Daedalus make wings for Icarus
f. (1) adverbial clause of time
(2) adverbial preposing
(3) coordination
(4) deletion
(5) infinitive complement
(6) indirect object preposing
(7) *that* clause complement
(8) possessive determiner
(9) personal pronominalization
(10) negation
(11) intensifier
g. causal clause, conditional clause, conjunction

5. a. 2, 26, 15, 19, 30, 7, 5, 24, 26
b. 4, 29, 31, 18, 35, 28, 24, 19, 24, 30, 12
c. 34, 6, 24, 18, 24, 2, 30, 24, 5, 35, 18, 24, 7, 10, 24
d. 6, 26, 24, 16, 1, 32, 5, 1, 29, 2, 30, 15, 9, 35, 24, 30
e. 23, 5, 24, 34, 9, 35, 24
f. 6, 26, 18, 35, 24, 30, 7, 28, 20, 24, 15
g. 36, 18, 37, 14, 35, 5, 18, 37, 27, 14, 35

6. *Syntactic Description*

a. Sentence Pattern: transitive verb pattern
Modalities: negation
Elaborations: prep phr modifier
that cl complement (2)
infinitive compl
Transformations: deletion (*that*)
pers pro (2)
contraction
intensifier
adv preposing

b. Sentence Pattern: transitive verb pattern
Modalities: yes-no question
Conjoinings: adv cl of time
Elaborations: *wh*-clause complement
Transformations: adv preposing
do-support
aux inversion
pers pro (2)

c. Sentence Pattern: linking verb pattern
intransitive verb pattern
Conjoinings: coordination (conjunction)
Elaborations: participle nominal
(possessive noun—*Nancy's*)
poss det
infinitive compl (purpose)
wh-clause complement
Transformations: pers pro (2)

Semantic Description

a. (one) girl think (something)
Experiencer—process—complement,
(one) girl be (in) the class
Entity—stative—location,
(one) girl be so smart
Entity—stative—intensifier—quality,
(one) girl study ever
Experiencer—process—frequency

b. (someone) know (something) (sometime)
Experiencer—process—complement—time,
(someone) be little
Entity—stative—size,
(someone) be president
Entity—stative—equivalent

c. Mother be upset (for some reason)
Entity—stative—condition—reason,
Nancy stay home
Entity—stative—location,
Mother go (to) room (for some reason)
Mover—action—location—reason,
Nancy have room
Possessor—process—patient,
Mother see (something)
Experiencer—process—complement,
Nancy feel (somehow)
Entity—stative—condition